Bibliographical Collection on the Garifuna People

Compilación Bibliográfica sobre el Nación Garífuna

Compilation Bibliographique sur le Nation Garifuna

Carlson John Tuttle

Introduction and Editing/ Présentation et édition/

Presentación y edición **Carlos Agudelo**

Published by *Producciones de la Hamaca*, Caye Caulker, Belize <producciones-hamaca.com>

ISBN: 978-976-8142-45-0

Published online by AFRODESC <ird.fr/afrodesc/>
Afrodescendants et esclavages: domination, identification et héritages dans les Amériques (15ème-21ème siècles):

Tuttle, Carlson (2012), Compilation bibliographique sur le peuple garifuna/ Compilación bibliográfica sobre el pueblo garífuna/ Bibliographical collection on the garifuna people. Carlos Agudelo (Ed.) Document de travail/Cuaderno de trabajo/ Working Paper 15. AFRODESC – EURESCL. <ird.fr/afrodesc/> France, Juin / Francia, Junio / France, June 2012

Table of Contents/ *Table de Matières* / *Indice de Materias*

Foreword

A bibliography is an indispensable tool for research. It guides the student to what has been written on a given topic and where it can be found. As a result, one can better fine tune what one should focus on for a given topic. In this regard, Carlson Tuttle has given anyone interested in Garifuna studies an invaluable source of assistance not previously available. He has made a compilation of almost 900 entries extending in time from the 1600s to 2012.

The length of time it took Carlson to make the list — a period of over thirty years — is only one indicator of the thoroughness he applied to the task. I have worked with him on several projects to know that his perfectionism in drawing up lists is second to none. As he drew closer to finishing this particular compilation he literally spent hours on end to make sure that he had the details correct for all the entries, and more especially, that he was not missing any.

The beneficiaries of Carlson's bibliography are persons and institutions dedicated to the study of the Central American-Caribbean subregion, the larger field of indigenous peoples in the Americas; and, of course, those primarily focusing on Garifuna people from the Eastern Caribbean, to Central America, and the North American diaspora. The bibliography shows that persons with such interest come from all over the world.

There is another beneficiary of this solid piece of scholarship. It is the village of Barranco. At a time when persons are travelling to sample the cultural gifts of the globe, this bibliography is a strong invitation to visitors to come to the village to see Carlson's collection and learn firsthand from him about the gems that he keeps unearthing.

Joseph O. Palacio

Benebu, Barranco

July, 2012.

Acknowledgements and Preface

I wish to first thank the ancestors for passing on their knowledge and experience which has allowed me to become who I am. Thanks to Odille Hoffman and Carlos Agudelo for suggesting this project, for their confidence in my ability to carry it out, and for their encouragement. I want to thank Dr. Joseph Palacio for his encouragement and for answering my many questions. I am grateful to Judy Lumb for her help in proofreading and editing the manuscript. And, especially, I want to thank all the librarians and archivists who have assisted me over the years, who are too numerous to name. Ann Kieffer has provided moral support and enthusiatic participation in my work. Lastly thanks to the Baranguna (Barranco's people) who have nurtured and encouraged me over the years.

Since my first visit to the Graduate Library at the University of Michigan in August of 1962 I have had a love affair with its stacks. Over the years I have spent many wonderful hours there. In 1985 while doing research on broom making in Belize, I found and read Douglas Taylor's *The Black Caribs of British Honduras*. This began the making of this bibliography. In 1989, after gathering numerous papers and books on Garifuna culture, I formally established Tuani Garifuna Tuba Liburu, an anthropological research library, in the Garifuna village of Barranco in which I am a resident.

Over the years I have visited many libraries and archives doing research and collecting material on Garifuna culture. Many authors have contributed papers and books, the Emory Whipple Library that was contributed by Emory's widow was a major addition in 1995. Over the years material has been collected from many disparate sources, school attendance records, government census records, church sacramental records, church correspondences, immigration records, government birth, marriage and death records, government land records and maps, government minute papers, and personal letters.

From this plethora of material this bibliography comes. The material included in this work is mainly academic books, papers and theses with an emphasis on printed material.

1

There are some popular works including novels and children's books. English language works are the majority with a large number in French and Spanish. In the last twenty years a number of works have been published in the German language. There is also a scattering of publications in other languages. Over the past forty years an increasing number of works have been authored by Garinagu, both academic and popular.

I am sure that I have missed some important citations, for which I apologize, but I need to stop somewhere and this is where it is. To communicate with the author write <carlsontuttle@gmail.com>.

Remerciements et Preface

Je souhaite d'abord remercier les ancêtres pour m'avoir transmis leurs connaissances et leur expérience afinde devenir qui je suis. Je remercie également Odile Hoffman et Carlos Agudelo de m'avoir proposé la réalisation de ce projet, de m'avoir accordé leur confiance et encouragé. Un grand merci au Dr Joseph Palacio pour son soutien et pour ses réponses à mes nombreuses questions ainsi qu'à Judy Lumb pour son aide dans la relecture et l'édition du manuscrit (basse de donnes Excel). Je tiens à remercier chaleureusement tous les bibliothécaires et les archivistes qui m'ont aidé, trop nombreux pour être tous nommés. Mes derniers remerciements s'adressent aux Baranguna, (habitants de Barranco) qui m'ont inspiré et encouragé durant toutes ces années.

Dès ma première visite à la Graduate Library de l'Université du Michigan durant le mois d'août 1962, je suis tombé amoureux de ses rayons. J'y ai passé de merveilleux moments au fil des ans. En 1985, alors que je menais des recherches sur la fabrication traditionnelle de balai au Bélize, j'ai trouvé et lu l'ouvrage de Douglas Taylor The Black Caribs of British Honduras. C'est à partir de cet écrit que la constitution de la bibliographie a commencé. En 1989, après avoir réuni de nombreux articles et ouvrages sur la culture garifuna, j'ai officiellement créé Tuani Garifuna Tuba Liburu, une bibliothèque de recherche anthropologique, dans mon village garifuna de résidence, Barranco.

Au fil des ans, je me suis rendu dans de nombreuses bibliothèques et centres d'archives dans le but de mener mes recherches et rassembler des articles et ouvrages sur la culture garifuna. De nombreux auteurs m'ont fait don de livres et d'articles et l'acquisition en 1995 de la bibliothèque d'Emory Whipple grâce au don la veuve d'Emory Whipple a contribué grandement à la constitution de la collection. D'autres documents ont été rassemblés à partir de sources variées comme le gouvernement (registres d'écoles et d'églises, recensements, registres d'immigration, de naissance, de mariage et de décès, cartographie étatique et des communiqués aux citoyens) ainsi que des lettres personnelles.

C'est à partir de cette pléthore de documents que la bibliographie est née. Elle contient principalement des ouvrages et des articles académiques, la priorité ayant été donnée au matériel imprimé. Elle comprend également des œuvres populaires comme des romans et des livres pour enfants. La plupart des documents sont en anglais mais l'on y trouve également de nombreuses œuvres publiées en français et en espagnol. Un certain nombre d'ouvrages datant de ces vingt dernières années a été publié en allemand. La compilation bibliographique liste un grand nombre d'ouvrages dans d'autres langues. De plus, ces quarante dernières années, un nombre grandissant d'ouvrages aussi bien académiques que populaires a été écrit par des Garifunas.

Je suis convaincu que j'ai oublié de citer bien d'autres contributions encore et je m'en excuse mais il fallait bien m'arrêter. Pour contacter l'auteur, écrire à: <carlsontuttle@gmail.co>.

Agradecimientos y Prefacio

Quiero agradecer primero a los ancestros por haberme transmitido sus conocimientos y su experiencia para que yo sea quien soy. Agradezco igualmente a Odile Hoffmann y a Carlos Agudelo por haberme propuesto la realización de este proyecto, haber tenido confianza en mí y animarme a hacerlo. Un gran agradecimiento al Dr. Joseph Palacio por su apoyo y por las respuestas a mis numerosas preguntas así como a Judy Lumb por su ayuda con la relectura y la edición de la base de datos Excel. Debo agradecer calurosamente a todos les bibliotecarios y archivistas que me han ayudado, muy numerosos para nombrarlos. Mis últimos agradecimientos se dirigen a los Baranguna (habitantes de Barranco) que me han inspirado y estimulado durante todos estos años.

Desde mi primera visita a la Graduate Library de la Universidad de Michigan durante el mes de agosto de 1962, me enamore de esos estantes. Allí pasé maravillosos momentos a los largo de los años. En 1985, mientras hacia investigaciones sobre la fabricación tradicional de la escoba en Belice, encontré la obra de Douglas Taylor, *The Black Caribs of British Honduras*. Es a partir de este escrito que la constitución de la bibliografía comenzó. En 1989 luego de haber reunido numerosos artículos y obras sobre la cultura garífuna, creé oficialmente Tuani Garifuna Tuba Liburu, una biblioteca de investigación antropológica, en mi pueblo garífuna de residencia, Barranco.

A lo largo de los años visité numerosas bibliotecas y centros de archivos con el objetivo de realizar mis investigaciones y reunir artículos y obras sobre la cultura garífuna. Varios autores me han obsequiado sus libros y artículos y la adquisición en 1995 de la biblioteca de Emory Whipple gracias a la donación de la viuda de Emory Whipple contribuyó mucho a la constitución de la colección. Otros documentos han sido reunidos a partir de fuentes diversas como los registros de escuelas y de iglesias, correspondencia de iglesias, censos, registros de inmigración, de nacimiento, de matrimonio y de fallecimientos, registros catastrales y cartografía, minutas gubernamentales y cartas personales.

Es a partir de esta plétora de documentos que la bibliografía nació. Ella contiene principalmente obras y artículos académicos, dándole la prioridad a material impreso. Ella incluye igualmente obras populares como novelas y libros para niños. La mayor parte de documentos están en inglés pero se encuentran también numerosas obras en francés y en español. Cierto número de trabajos que datan de los últimos veinte años han sido escritos en alemán. La compilación bibliográfica incluye muchas obras en otras lenguas. Además, en los últimos cuarenta años un importante número de trabajos tanto académicos como populares han sido escritos por Garífunas.

Estoy convencido que he dejado de citar muchas contribuciones importantes y les pido mis excusas pero tenia que para en algún momento. Para tomar contacto con el autor escribir a <carlsontuttle@gmail.com>.

Introduction

In America, the Garifuna[1] are distinguished from other populations with sub-Saharan African heritage, also called "black populations," which include Afro-Americans with national variations as Afro-Colombians, Afro-Brazilians, Afro-Cubans, and other recent Afro-descendants. The Garifuna originate from a mix of African and Carib and Arawak Indians from the Lesser Antilles during the colonial period from the 16th to 18th centuries. The English exiled the Garifuna to Central America by the end of the 18th century. After their exile, the Garifuna settled in Trujillo, Honduras, then spread transnationally along the coasts of Honduras, Guatemala, Belize and Nicaragua. This has resulted in a multifaceted identification based upon their national, transnational, black, and indigenous identities. From the middle of the 20th century, the Garifuna started to migrate to the United States. Despite these vast changes in settlement and their diverse national and linguistic contexts, the Garifuna have preserved many unique cultural traditions, such as, their language, spirituality, music, dance and diet.

This bibliography on the Garifuna was published as part of the research, documentation, and dissemination of information by the AFRODESC and EURESCL programs. Part of the work was done in Central America and is still ongoing due to much continuing interest in the Garifuna culture.

The author of this work is Carlson Tuttle, an expert who has documented many aspects of the society, language, and culture of the Garifuna. Based in Belize for more than 30 years, Carlson has engaged in the long and difficult task of compiling references from various disciplines since 1985. We believe that experts and others interested in the Garifuna will find this bibliography to be an extremely valuable resource.

---

1 The word "Garifuna" comes from Karina in Arawak language and means "yucca eaters". Some authors differentiated the word "Garifuna" as singular to designate individuals and the language, and the term "Garinagu" or "Garifunas" as plural to designate the population. We notice in the references of this collection, different forms are used as well as the expression "Black Caribs".

Odile Offmann, a researcher for AFRODESC-EURESCL[2], and I had the opportunity to meet Carlson. He was introduced to us by Joseph Palacio, our Garifuna colleague from Belize, who is an expert anthropologist on the Garifuna. In 2009 we visited Carlson in his house-library, where he showed us part of his documentary work, which included documents of diverse formats: printed books, papers, lists, and computerized archives.

As part of the AFRODESC-EURESCL programs, we had already published bibliographical collections and anthologies of works poorly disseminated on studies of African descendants in Mexico and Central America, as well as Belize. Due to the relevance of Carlson's empirical work, we proposed the systematization of his collection of documentary and bibliographical data in order to publish and make it accessible for researchers and the Garifuna people. Carlson accepted and we gradually started working on the project.

The collection is composed of 888 entries of documents published between 1665 and 2012. Carlson has classified the documents in the following categories: History; Ethno-history; Anthropology; Linguistics; Spirituality; Music, Dance and Arts; Literature; Health and Medicine; Education; and Tourism. There are 331 book entries, 102 university works that are primarily doctoral theses, 452 articles from scientific journals, and a few other documents that are hard to access, such as, conference proceedings, diverse reports, and releases.

By analyzing the references in this bibliography, we can draw several conclusions. Since their origins as a people on the island of Saint Vincent, the Garifuna strongly attracted attention from missionaries, travelers and colonial officials. The first references of the Garifuna people are from the French and British in the 17th century. Among these references are the chronicles and linguistic studies of Abbot Raymond Breton

2 AFRODESC – Afro-descendants et esclavages: domination, identification et héritages dans les Amériques, program of the National Research Agency – ANR of France <ird.fr/afrodesc/>. EURESCL - Slave Trade, Slavery, Abolitions and their Legacies in European Histories and Identities, program of the European Union <eurescl.eu/>.

(*Dictionnaire Caraïbe-Français et Grammaire Caraïbe*). During the 19th century, the Garifuna people were also mentioned in the travel writings, linguistics studies and colonial reports, not only from the Lesser Antilles but also from the new settlements in Central America. During the same century, historical works were mostly written by the English and the first references by authors from the United States were published. By the end of the 19th century, the first anthropological writings were published.

Despite the classification by discipline of this collection, the boundaries that separate the disciplines were extremely porous between the 17th and 19th centuries and several works could be considered as part of history but also of anthropology, ethno-history, or geography.

Of the 590 references published in the 20th century, only 40 are from the first half, while the other 550 works were published after 1950. The decade of the 1950s is when the first doctoral theses about the Garifuna appeared. Of particular interest are *The Consanguineal Household among the Black Carib of Central America*, the doctoral thesis of the North-American anthropologist Nancie Gonzalez, (one of the most prolific authors on the subject), and *The Black Carib of Honduras*, the work of the Brazilian anthropologist Ruy Galvao de Andrade Cohelo. Also during this time the English linguist and anthropologist Douglas MacRae Taylor wrote one of the major works on Garifuna, *The Black Caribs of British Honduras*. The first edition of Taylor's masterpiece was published in 1951 and the last in 1988. His work is mainly composed of articles published in scientific journals of anthropology and linguistics.

Until the 1970s, there were very few references from Central American authors and the few publications in Spanish are translations of works of North American and European authors. This is probably due to the poor development of social sciences in the academic communities of Central American countries at this time. Between 1970 and 1980, the number of publications doubled compared to the previous decade, from 46 to 105. During this period, we see emerging Belizean intellectuals in the work of anthropologist Joseph Palacio (1973) and linguist/political leader Roy Cayetano (1977) as well as the publication of a Garifuna-Spanish dictionary by the Honduran essayist Humberto Rivera y Morillo (1977).

During the 1980s, the publications continued to increase, and more university works (primarily masters and doctoral theses from universities in the United States) were published. As indigenous cultural matters gained more credibility within the international community, studies of specific aspects of the Garifuna culture, such as their language and religiosity, kept increasing. In 1985, the Guatemalan anthropologist Alfonso Arrivillaga published his first work on the Garifuna culture in Guatemala. From the end of the 1980s to the beginning of the 1990s, the issues of the black populations in Latin America became more visible as the ethno-racial diversity in several countries of the region was recognized. This was the beginning of the so-called multicultural or recognition policies. This process had a direct impact on the number of works published on the Garifuna.

Between 1990 and the end of the compilation (2011), the number of references doubled compared to the previous two decades. In 2001 UNESCO recognized the Garifuna culture as a masterpiece of the oral and intangible heritage of humanity. This was another contributing factor that stimulated research and publication of more works on the subject. About 25 percent of this collection is from the period 2000-2012.

From this period, the anthropologic and linguistic works outnumber the rest. Indeed, among the cultural aspects of the Garifuna people, their language has aroused the most attention. After referring to the pioneering masterpieces of the Father Raymond Breton and Douglas MacRae Taylor, we have to mention the French linguist Sybille de Pury Toumi who published one of her studies in the 1990s. In anthropology, the work of the Belizean Garifuna anthropologist Joseph Palacio published in 2005, *The Garifuna, a Nation Across Borders: Essays in Social Anthropology*, is one of the greatest collections of works on this subject. The Guatemalan Alfonso Arrivillaga published most of his works during this period. The works of two Americans must be mentioned for their studies. Mark

Anderson wrote *Black and Indigenous. Garifuna activism and Consumer Culture in Honduras* (2009); Sarah England wrote *Creating a Global Garífuna Nation. The Transnationalization of Race, Class, Gender and Politics in the Garífuna Diaspora* (2000). This period is marked by the publication of works written by intellectuals and political activists. After mentioning the Belizeans Roy Cayetano and Justo Flores, we can add the Hondureans Salvador Suazo, Crisanto Meléndez, Santos Centeno, and Virgilio López García as well as the Guatemalan Mario Ellington. Honduran Historians Darío Euraque and Jorge Amaya can be noted in this period of great publications.

By observing the references of this collection we see another interesting fact: the titles of the works from the collection reveal changes in identification of the Garifuna. The first references (from the 16th to the beginning of the 20th century) use the generic "Caribs". The first appearance of "Black Caribs" is in the work of Eduard Conzemus in 1928. He also uses in parentheses the term "Garif". In his numerous and relevant works, Taylor strictly uses the term "Black Caribs," as did Cohelo and Nancie Gonzalez to mention some of the greatest authors. In 1974, the term "Garifuna" was used for the first time (along with "Black Caribs" in parentheses) in the writings of geographer William Davidson, who strictly used in his last works the term "Garifuna." By the end of the 1980s, the use of "Black Caribs" had almost disappeared. One of the exceptions is the doctoral thesis of the French Nicolas Rey, *Quand la Révolution, aux Amériques, était Nègre… Caraïbes Noirs, Negros Franceses et autres «Oubliés» de l'Histoire* published in 2005. In an article published in 1976, Nancie Gonzalez discussed the change of self-representation of the Garifuna and stated the transformation from "Black Caribs" to "Garifuna" as a process of ethnic identification corresponding to the politicization of the identity, influenced by the experience of the American Indian and the Civil Rights movements in the United States. Thus, there is a confluence in the process of transformation between the scientific studies and self-representations of these populations. This was reinforced in the 1990s with the entry of recognition policies and the main role played by the black or Afro-descendent populations, such as the Garifuna.

Finally, when we look at the distribution of the references listed by discipline in Carlson's collection, we notice that half of them are classified as belonging to Anthropology. If we add Ethno-history; Linguistics; Spirituality; Music, Dance and Arts, Literature, Education, Tourism, and those of Health and Medicine that are generally linked to Anthropology, we realize how much attention the culture of these populations attracted. The rest of the references, that is 10 percent of the collection, are history works which can also be linked to culture. Most the works on contemporary issues could also be classified in sociology or political sciences.

Among the 331 publications, 155 (47%) were published in the United States while the other 54 percent were published in Latin America (40%) and Europe (13%). Within total of 192 university works, 62 are doctoral theses and 37 are Masters or Bachelors. Ninety percent of these documents were published in the United States. The vast majority (85%) of the periodical articles and other references (455) were published in English.

Universities in the United States are the predominant publishers. However, the academic reference started to diversify gradually from the 1980s onwards, especially with the publications in the Central American countries with a Garifuna population (mainly Belize and Honduras).

This collection of works published from the 17th to the 21st century in different geographical places and in distinct formats meets the criteria of a great bibliography that is essentially different and little known by experts and other people interested in the subject, not to mention people interested in black populations who are unaware of the Garifuna. That is why the programs AFRODESC-EURESCL are glad to help publish and disseminate the work of Carlson Tuttle. The collection is available in a PDF format on the website <ird.fr/afrodesc>.

Anyone interested in receiving the collection in a database format (which will arrange the references alphabetically by author, chronologically or by place of publication—books and theses), may request by an email to <ceagarifuna@

gmail.com>. Please indicate the email address to be used for delivery.

As coordinator of this editorial work, I cannot conclude without expressing my gratitude to Odile Hoffmann for her vital support and participation. I would also like to thank my daughter Mayra Agudelo for her translation in French, English and Spanish of this introduction as well as Carlson Tuttle's biography, acknowledgements, and preface.

Carlos Agudelo

Sociologist - Researcher AFRODESC-EURESCL

Associated Member URMIS

Migrations and Society Research Unit <www.unice.fr/urmis/>

Présentation

En Amérique, les garifuna[3] possèdent des singularités qui les distinguent des autres populations d'origine africaine (sub-saharienne) ou que l'on appelle également populations noires, afro-américaines (avec ses variantes nationales du type afro-colombiennes, afro-brésiliennes, afro-cubaines, etc.) ou plus récemment les *afro-descendants*. Issue d'un métissage entre Africains et indiens caraïbes et arawaks dans les Antilles mineures durant la période coloniale (au XVIe et au XVIIIe siècle), leur spécificité repose bien sur l'histoire de leur origine. Vers la fin du XVIIIe siècle, les garifuna sont déportés par les Anglais en Amérique centrale. Depuis leur premier peuplement sur le continent à Trujillo, Honduras, le peuple garifuna commence à s'installer de manière, que l'on dirait aujourd'hui, transnationale sur les côtes caraïbes du Honduras, Guatemala, Belize et Nicaragua. C'est ainsi qu'est déclenché le processus d'identification multiple entre l'identité nationale, transnationale, noire y indienne. À partir du milieu du XXe siècle, les garifuna commencent à migrer en grand nombre aux États-Unis. Malgré ces dynamiques de mobilité et de peuplement dans des contextes nationaux et linguistiques très divers, ils préservent, certaines caractéristiques culturelles comme la langue, la religiosité, la musique, la danse et les traditions alimentaires.

La publication de cette compilation bibliographique sur les garifuna s'inscrit dans le cadre des travaux de recherche, de documentation et de diffusion des programmes AFRODESC et EURESCL[4]. Une partie de ces travaux a été réalisée en

---

3 Le mot garifuna désignant les individus ou la population vient du terme karina en langue arawak qui signifie « mangeurs de manioc ». Quelques auteurs différencient l'usage du mot garifuna au singulier pour désigner les individus et la langue, de l'usage du mot garinagu ou garifunas au pluriel pour parler de la population. On remarquera que dans les références de la compilation, toutes ces différentes formes sont utilisées, tout comme l'expression « Caraïbes noirs »".

4 AFRODESC-EURESCL – Afro-descendants et esclavages : domination, identification et héritages dans les Amériques, programme de l'Agence Nationale de Recherche – ANR de France <ird.fr/afrodesc/>. EURESCL – Slave, Trade, Slavery, Abolitions and their legacies in European Histories and Identities, programme de l'Union européenne <eurescl.eu/>.

Amérique centrale et d'autres projets sur les garifuna sont toujours en cours.

L'auteur de ce travail est Carlson Tuttle, documentaliste et spécialiste des questions socio-culturelles garifuna. Installé au Belize depuis plus de 30 ans, Carlson Tuttle a réalisé une compilation de références multidisciplinaires qu'il a commencé en 1985, comme lui-même le décrit ci-dessous. Ce travail de longue haleine possède à nos yeux une valeur inestimable pour les spécialistes et les personnes intéressées par le sujet.

Odile Hoffmann, chercheure pour les programmes AFRODESC et EURESCL, et moi-même avons eu la chance de rencontrer Carlson Tuttle grâce à notre collègue anthropologue garifuna belizéen, Joseph Palacio. Nous lui avons rendu visite à Barranco, Belize, dans sa maison-bibliothèque où il nous a montré une partie de son travail documentaire qui, à cette époque (2009), comprenait divers formats (papier, listes variées d'archives informatisés etc.).

Nous avions déjà publié, dans le cadre des programmes AFRODESC-EURESCL, des compilations bibliographiques et des anthologies de travaux peu diffusés sur des populations d'origine africaine au Mexique et en Amérique centrale. Face à la valeur d'un tel travail, nous avons proposé à Carlson de systématiser sa compilation d'informations documentaires et bibliographiques afin de l'éditer et de la rendre accessible aussi bien aux chercheurs qu'aux propres garifunas. Carlson a accepté notre proposition et nous avons dès lors commencé la réalisation de ce projet.

La compilation est composée de 888 titres, publiés entre 1665 et 2012 et classés par Carlson Tuttle dans les domaines suivants : histoire, ethnohistoire, anthropologie, linguistique, spiritualité, musique danse et arts, littérature, santé et médecine, éducation et tourisme. Parmi ces titres, 331 correspondent à des livres et 102 à des travaux universitaires (essentiellement des thèses doctorales). On y trouve également 455 articles de publications périodiques (revues scientifiques) et autres documents difficilement accessibles (actes de colloques, rapports divers, communications).

En observant les références bibliographiques, plusieurs conclusions peuvent être tirées. Dès leur « naissance » en tant que peuple sur l'île de Saint Vincent, les garifuna ont suscité un vif intérêt chez les missionnaires, voyageurs et fonctionnaires coloniaux. Au XVIIe siècle, l'existence des garifuna est évoquée pour la première fois dans des chroniques d'auteurs anglais et français. Parmi ces œuvres, on distingue les chroniques et travaux de linguistique du Père Raymond Breton (*Dictionnaire Caraïbe-Français et Grammaire Caraïbe*). Au XIXe siècle, les récits de voyages, études linguistiques et rapports coloniaux mentionnent aussi bien les garifuna vivant dans les Antilles mineures que ceux installés dans les nouveaux lieux de peuplement en Amérique centrale. Durant ce même siècle, les travaux d'histoire sont majoritairement écrits par les Anglais. C'est également à cette époque qu'apparaissent les premières références d'auteurs étatsuniens. À la fin du XIXe siècle, les premiers écrits d'anthropologie sont rédigés.

Il faut souligner que les frontières qui séparent les catégories élaborées pour cette bibliographie, sont extrêmement poreuses et que, notamment pour les documents publiés entre le XVIIe et le XIXe siècle, plusieurs travaux peuvent être considérés comme appartenant aussi bien à l'histoire qu'à l'anthropologie, l'ethnohistoire ou la géographie.

Parmi les 590 références de la compilation publiées au XXe siècle, seules 40 datent de la première moitié du siècle alors que 550 correspondent aux travaux réalisés après 1950. C'est dans les années 1950 que l'on voit apparaître les premières thèses doctorales sur les garifuna, parmi lesquelles se distinguent celle de l'anthropologue nord-américaine Nancie Gonzalez (une des auteures les plus prolifiques sur le sujet), *The Consanguineal Household among the Black Carib of Central America*, et celle de l'anthropologue brésilien Ruy Galvao de Andrade Cohelo, *The Black Carib of Honduras*. En 1951, le linguiste et anthropologue anglais Douglas MacRae Taylor écrit l'une des principales œuvres de référence sur les garifuna, *The Black Caribs of British Honduras*. La première édition de l'œuvre de Taylor date de 1935 et la dernière de 1988. Son œuvre est composée principalement d'articles de publications scientifiques d'anthropologie et de linguistique.

Jusqu'aux années 1970, on ne trouve que très peu de références d'auteurs d'Amérique centrale et les rares publications en espagnol sont des traductions des travaux d'auteurs nord-américains et européens. Ceci est probablement dû au faible développement des sciences sociales dans les milieux universitaires des pays d'Amérique centrale jusqu'à cette époque. Entre 1970 et 1980, le nombre de publications double par rapport à la décennie précédente et passe de 46 à 105. Durant cette période on distingue les travaux de l'anthropologue Joseph Palacio (1973) et de l'intellectuel et dirigeant politique Roy Cayetano (1977), tous deux Belizéens, ainsi que la publication d'un dictionnaire garifuna-espagnol par l'essayiste hondurien Humberto Rivera y Morillo (1977).

Dans les années 1980, la tendance ne faiblit pas avec des publications et des travaux universitaires (masters et thèses doctorales principalement d'universités nord-américaines). Les problématiques culturelles « indiennes » obtiennent plus de crédibilité au sein de la communauté internationale et les études sur des aspects spécifiques de la culture garifuna tels que la langue ou la religiosité ne cessent de se multiplier. En 1985, l'anthropologue guatémaltèque Alfonso Arrivillaga publie son premier ouvrage sur la culture garifuna au Guatemala. À partir de la fin des années 1980 et du début des années 1990, un processus de visibilisation des problématiques des populations noires en Amérique latine se met en place, dans un contexte de changements institutionnels en matière de reconnaissance de la diversité ethnoraciale dans plusieurs pays de la région. C'est effectivement à cette époque que surgissent les politiques multiculturelles et de reconnaissance. Ce processus aura un impact direct sur le nombre de publications sur les garifuna.

Entre 1990 et la fin de la compilation (2012), le nombre de références double encore par rapport aux deux décennies précédentes. L'établissement en 2001 par l'Unesco de la culture garifuna comme patrimoine intangible de l'humanité sera un autre facteur qui a stimulé la réalisation des recherches et des publications sur le sujet. En effet, près d'un quart des références de cette compilation correspond à la période 2000-2012.

16

Durant cette période, les études anthropologiques et linguistiques restent les plus nombreuses et la langue garifuna est un aspect de la culture qui a suscité un grand intérêt. Après l'œuvre pionnière du Père Breton et celle de Taylor, l'ouvrage de la linguiste française Sybille de Pury Toumi est publié dans les années 1990. En anthropologie, l'anthropologue garifuna bélizéen Joseph Palacio, publie en 2005, l'un des travaux collectifs les plus importants sur le sujet : *The Garifuna, a Nation Across Borders: Essays in Social Anthropology*. Le Guatémaltèque Alfonso Arrivillaga publie également la plupart de ses ouvrages durant cette période. Les travaux des Étatsuniens Mark Anderson et Sarah England sont à citer également, notamment deux de leurs principales études respectives : *Black and Indigenous. Garifuna activism and Consumer Culture in Honduras* (2009) et *Creating a Global Garífuna Nation. The Transnationalization of Race, Class, Gender and Politics in the Garífuna Diaspora* (2000). Cette période est également marquée par la publication d'œuvres d'intellectuels et d'activistes garifuna. Si l'on évoque la contribution des Bélizéens Roy Cayetano et de Justo Flores, on peut mentionner également Salvador Suazo, Crisanto Meléndez, Santos Centeno et Virgilio López García, tous Honduriens ainsi que le Guatémaltèque Mario Ellington. Pendant ces années, on remarque également les travaux des historiens honduriens Darío Euraque et Jorge Amaya.

L'observation des références de cette compilation met en exergue une autre donnée intéressante. En effet, les titres des travaux que contient la compilation dévoilent les transformations des formes d'identification et de représentation des garifuna. Les premières réferences (du XVIe siècle au début du XXe) utilisent la dénomination générique *Caraïbes*. En 1928, le terme *Caraïbes noirs* apparaît pour la première fois dans l'œuvre d'Eduard Conzemius qui utilise également entre parenthèses le terme «Garif». Dans ses nombreux et importants travaux, Doublas MacRaeTaylor utilise uniquement le terme *Caraïbes noirs*, comme le fait Ruy Galvao de Andrade Cohelo ou Nancie González pour ne mentionner que certains grands auteurs. En 1974, le terme *garifuna* est utilisé pour la première fois (bien qu'accompagné de « Caraïbes noirs » entre parenthèses) dans l'œuvre du géographe William Davidson, qui optera exclusivement dans ses derniers travaux pour le terme *garifuna*. Vers la fin des années 1980, l'usage de "Caraïbes noirs" a pratiquement disparu. Une des exceptions notables est la publication en 2005 de la thèse doctorale du Français Nicolas Rey, *Quand la Révolution, aux Amériques, était Nègre... Caraïbes Noirs, Negros Franceses et autres « Oubliés » de l'Histoire*. Dans un article publié en 1976, Nancie González parle justement de la transformation de la forme d'auto-représentation chez les garifuna et considère le passage de "Caraïbes noirs" à "Garifunas" comme un processus d'ethnicisation qui correspondrait à une politisation de l'identité, influencée par l'expérience du mouvement indien ainsi que du mouvement noir aux États-Unis. Il y a donc une confluence dans le processus de transformation en termes de dénomination entre les études scientifiques et les auto-représentations de ces populations. Cette tendance sera confirmée dans les années 1990 avec l'avènement des politiques de reconnaissance et le rôle principal qu'y joueront les populations noires ou d'origine africaine, et parmi elles les garifuna.

Finalement, lorsque l'on observe la répartition par domaine des références de la compilation de Carlson Tuttle, on constate que la moitié appartient au domaine de l'anthropologie. Si l'on y additionne l'ethnohistoire, la linguistique, la spiritualité, la musique, danse et arts, la littérature ainsi que l'éducation et le tourisme sans oublier la santé et la médecine (généralement un lien entre l'anthropologie, les sciences médicales et la biologie), on constate que l'intérêt suscité par la culture de ces populations est considérable. Les références restantes, soit 10% de la compilation, correspondent à des travaux d'histoire dont la plupart sont extrêmement liés à la culture. Il faut également souligner que plusieurs travaux portant sur des problématiques contemporaines pourraient appartenir également à la sociologie ou aux sciences politiques.

Des 331 livres de la compilation, 155 (47%) ont été publiés aux États-Unis alors que les 54% restants conrrespondent à des publications en Amérique latine (40%) et en Europe (13%). En ce qui concerne les travaux universitaires, sur un ensemble de 192 références, 62 sont des thèses doctorales ; 37 des masters et licences ; 90% de ces documents proviennent d'universités aux États-Unis. Pour les articles de revues et autres références (455), l'anglais est la langue principale de publication (85%). En matière de travaux universitaires, on note la prédominance des éditions universitaires des États-Unis. Néanmoins, les références commencent progressivement à se diversifier à partir des années 1980, notamment avec l'apparition de publications réalisées dans les pays d'Amérique centrale ayant une population garifuna (principalement au Belize et au Honduras).

Cette compilation de travaux réalisés au fil des siècles (du XVIIᵉ au XXIᵉ siècle), dans divers espaces géographiques et sous de multiples formats permet de constater l'existence d'une production bibliographique considérable, mais dispersée et partiellement connue des spécialistes et autres personnes interessées sur le sujet ; sans parler des personnes qui s'intéressent aux populations noires d'autres régions du monde et qui ne connaissent pas l'existence des garifuna. C'est pourquoi les programmes AFRODESC – EURESCL, fidèles à leurs objectifs, se réjouissent de contribuer à l'édition et à la diffusion du travail de Carlson Tuttle.

Cette compilation est disponible sous format PDF sur le site <ird.fr/afrodesc>.

Les personnes souhaitant recevoir la compilation sous un format de base de données (par exemple pour classer les références par ordre alphabétique des auteurs, par ordre chronologique ou par lieu d'édition – livres et thèses -) devront en faire la demande à <ceagarifuna@gmail.com> en indiquant le courrier électronique par lequel elles désirent recevoir le fichier.

En tant que coordinateur de ce travail d'édition, je ne peux conclure cette présentation sans mentionner le soutien et la participation d'Odile Hoffmann qui furent cruciaux pour sa finalisation. Je remercie également ma fille Mayra Agudelo pour la traduction français-espagnol-anglais de cette présentation ainsi que de celle de Carlson Tuttle.

Carlos Agudelo
Sociologue- Chercheur AFRODESC-EURESCL, Chercheur associé URMIS
Unité de Recherche Migrations et Société <unice.fr/urmis>

Presentación

En América, entre los grupos humanos de origen africano (sub-sahariano) o también llamados poblaciones negras, afroamericanas (con sus declinaciones nacionales – afrocolombianos, afrobrasileños, afrocubanos, etc. etc.) o más recientemente afrodescendientes, los garífuna[5] tienen connotaciones especiales. En su historia y devenir actual llama la atención su origen en el mestizaje entre africanos e indígenas caribes y arawaks en las Antillas menores durante el periodo colonial (siglos XVI al XVIII). Los garifuna son deportados por los ingleses hacia América Central a finales del siglo XVIII. Desde su asentamiento inicial en Trujillo, Honduras, esta población inicia su asentamiento, que actualmente llamariamos transnacional, en las costas caribes de lo que hoy son Honduras, Guatemala, Belice y Nicaragua. Ellos van construyendo un proceso de identificación múltiple entre lo nacional, lo transnacional, lo negro y lo indígena. A partir de mediados del siglo XX los garífuna inician una importante migración hacia los Estados Unidos. En medio de estas dinámicas de movilidad y poblamiento, en contextos nacionales y liguisticos diversos, ellos mantienen en un proceso complejo y dinámico ciertas características culturales tales como su lengua, su religiosidad, la música, la danza y sus tradiciones alimentarias.

La publicación de la presente compilación bibliográfica sobre los garífuna se inscribe en el marco de los trabajos de investigación, documentación y difusión realizados por los programas AFRODESC y EURESCL[6]. Una parte de este trabajo se ha realizado en América Central y el interés por los pueblos garífuna hace parte de investigaciones que aun están en curso.

5 La palabra garífuna con la cual se puede nombrar a los individuos o al grupo de población viene del término Karina en lengua arawak que significaría "comedores de yuca". Algunos autores diferencian la palabra garífuna en singular para nombrar los individuos y la lengua mientras que el grupo de población se le llama garinagu o garífunas en plural. En las referencias de la presente compilación se usan las diferentes formas así como la apelación de "caribes negros".
6 AFRODESC- Afrodescendientes y esclavitudes: dominación, identificación y herencias en las Américas, programa de la Agencia Nacional de Investigación – ANR de Francia <ird.fr/afrodesc/>. EURESCL- Slave Trade, Slavery, Abolitions and their Legacies in European Histories and Identities, programa de la Union europea <eurescl.eu/>.

El autor de este trabajo, Carlson Tuttle es especialista y documentalista de las problemáticas sociales y culturales de los Garífuna. Radicado en Belice desde hace más de treinta años, Carlson ha realizado esta recopilación de referencias multidisciplinarias desde 1985, como él mismo lo describe en su prefacio. Ha sido un trabajo de largo aliento que consideramos será de gran valor para los especialistas e interesados en el tema.

Con Odile Hoffmann, investigadora de AFRODESC y EURESCL, tuvimos la oportunidad de conocer personalmente a Carlson, a través de nuestro colega, el antropólogo garífuna de Belice, Joseph Palacio. Lo visitamos en Barranco – Belice, en su casa-biblioteca donde nos mostró parte de su trabajo documental que en ese momento (2009) se encontraba disperso en varios formatos (impresos, listas varias en archivos informatizados, etc.).

En los programas AFRODESC-EURESCL teníamos ya antecedentes de publicaciones de compilaciones bibliográficas y antologías de trabajos poco difundidos sobre estudios de poblaciones de origen africano en México y América Central. Ante la relevancia del trabajo que de forma empírica venía realizando Carlson, le propusimos efectuar una sistematización de sus recopilaciones de información documental y bibliográfica para editarla difundirla y volverla accesible tanto a los investigadores como a los propios garífuna. Carlson aceptó nuestra propuesta y a partir de esta fecha, el trabajo comenzó a realizarse gradualmente.

La compilación está compuesta por 888 entradas y registra trabajos desde 1665 a 2012 clasificados en las siguientes disciplinas: historia, etnohistoria, antropología, lingüística, espiritualidad, música danza y artes, literatura, salud y medicina, educación y turismo. 331 entradas corresponden a libros, 102 a trabajos universitarios, mayoritariamente tesis de doctorado y 455 son artículos en publicaciones periódicas (revistas científicas) et otros documentos difícilmente accesibles (actas de coloquios, informes, ponencias, y otros formatos).

Una mirada a estas referencias bibliográficas permite inferir algunas reflexiones. Desde su proceso de gestación como pueblo en la isla de San Vicente, los garífuna despertaron el interés de misioneros, viajeros, funcionarios coloniales. Las primeras referencias francesas e inglesas datan del siglo XVII. Se distinguen las crónicas y trabajos de lingüística del abad Raymond Breton (Dictionnaire Caraïbe-Français et Grammaire Caraïbe). Para el siglo XIX siguen sobresaliendo las narraciones de viaje, los estudios de la lengua y los informes coloniales que se refieren tanto a las Antillas menores como a los nuevos asentamientos en América Central. En este siglo predominan los trabajos de historia realizados por ingleses y surgen las primeras referencias de autores estadounidenses. A finales de este siglo XIX aparecen los primeros escritos de antropología.

Hay que señalar que aunque en la presente compilación se realizó una clasificación por disciplinas, las fronteras entre ellas, en particular entre los siglos XVII y XIX son bastante porosas y varios de los trabajos podrían considerarse tanto de historia como de antropología, etnohistoria o geografía.

De las 590 referencias registradas para el siglo XX, tan sólo 40 conciernen a la primera mitad y 550 corresponden a trabajos realizados a partir de 1950. En esta década de los 1950 se realizan las primeras tesis doctorales sobre los garífuna. Se destacan las de la antropóloga norteamericana Nancie Gonzalez (una de las autoras mas prolíficas sobre el tema), The Consanguineal Household among the Black Carib of Central America y la del antropólogo brasilero Ruy Galvao de Andrade Cohelo, The Black Carib of Honduras. En 1951, el lingüista y antropólogo inglés, Douglas MacRae Taylor escribe una de las principales obras de referencia sobre los garífuna, The Black Caribs of British Honduras. La obra de Taylor comienza a ser publicada en 1935 y se extiende hasta 1988. Está constituida fundamentalmente de artículos en publicaciones científicas de antropología y lingüística.

Hasta los años 1970 encontraremos muy pocas referencias de autores centroamericanos y las pocas que se registran en español corresponden a traducciones de trabajos realizados por autores norteamericanos o europeos. Esto se relaciona seguramente con el poco desarrollo de las ciencias sociales en el medio universitario de los países centroamericanos hasta ese periodo. Durante la década 1970-1980 se duplican las publicaciones en relación con el decenio anterior (de 46 referencias a 105). Se destacan los trabajos del antropólogo Joseph Palacio (1973) y del intelectual y dirigente político Roy Cayetano (1977), ambos beliceños, y la publicación de un diccionario garífuna-español por el ensayista hondureño Humberto Rivera y Morillo (1977).

En los años 1980 continua una tendencia al aumento de publicaciones y la realización de trabajos universitarios (masters y doctorados, principalmente de universidades norteamericanas). Las problemáticas indígenas adquieren más relevancia en la opinión pública internacional y los estudios sobre aspectos específicos de la cultura garífuna, tales como su lengua y su religiosidad siguen incrementándose. En 1985 el antropólogo guatemalteco Alfonso Arrivillaga hace su primera publicación sobre la cultura garífuna en Guatemala. A finales de esta década y principios de los años 1990 se va gestar un proceso de visibilización de las problemáticas de los pueblos negros en América latina en el marco de los cambios institucionales en materia de reconocimiento de la diversidad etnoracial que se produce en varios países de la región. Es la llegada de las llamadas políticas multiculturales o de reconocimiento. Este proceso va a influir directamente en un nuevo aumento de publicaciones sobre los garífuna.

Entre 1990 y la finalización de esta recopilación (2012) se doblaron el número de referencias con respecto a las dos décadas anteriores. La declaración en 2001 de la cultura garífuna como patrimonio intangible de la humanidad por parte de la Unesco será otro factor que estimula la realización de investigaciones y de publicaciones sobre este tema. Prácticamente un cuarto de las referencias de esta compilación corresponde al periodo 2000-2012.

Durante estos años han continuado predominando los estudios antropológicos y de lingüística. En efecto, la lengua garífuna ha despertado un interés relevante entre los aspectos de la cultura de este grupo de población. Ya mencionábamos la obra pionera del abad Breton y los trabajos de Taylor, en los años 1990 se distingue la obra de la lingüista francesa Sybille de Pury Toumi. En antropología se afianza la obra del antropólogo garífuna de Belice Joseph Palacio quien edita en 2005 uno de los trabajos colectivos más importantes sobre este tema, *The Garífuna, a Nation Across Borders: Essays in Social Anthropology*. El guatemalteco Alfonso Arrivillaga también produce la mayor parte de su obra en estos años. Igualmente se distinguen los trabajos de los estadounidenses Mark Anderson y Sarah England. Dos de sus trabajos más importantes son respectivamente *Black and Indigenous. Garífuna activism and Consumer Culture in Honduras* (2009) y Creating a Global Garífuna Nation. *The Transnationalization of Race, Class, Gender and Politics in the Garífuna Diaspora* (2000). Otro elemento que se puede resaltar para este periodo es la publicación de obras de intelectuales y activistas garífunas. Además de los trabajos de Roy Cayetano y Justo Flores en Belice, podemos mencionar a Salvador Suazo, Crisanto Meléndez, Santos Centeno y Virgilio López García de Honduras y Mario Ellington de Guatemala. Se destacan igualmente los trabajos de los historiadores hondureños Darío Euraque y Jorge Amaya.

Un aspecto general interesante que se puede observar en las referencias de esta compilación es el hecho de que los títulos de los trabajos registrados muestran igualmente las transformaciones en la forma de identificación y de representación de los garífuna. Las primeras referencias (siglos XVI a principios del XX) utilizan la denominación genérica de Caribes. La primera referencia a Caribes negros se encuentra en el trabajo de Eduard Conzemius en 1928, quien también coloca entre paréntesis el termino « Garif ». Los numerosos e importantes trabajos de Taylor van utilizar solamente la denominación de Caribes negros, igualmente es el caso de Cohelo o de Nancie González para mencionar solo algunos de los autores más relevantes. En 1974 aparece la primera referencia con el termino « garífuna » (pero acompañado de « Caribes negros» entre paréntesis) en la obra del geógrafo William Davidson quien en sus últimos trabajos opta por el uso exclusivo del termino garífuna. Hacia finales de los años 1980 el uso de « Caribes negros » había prácticamente desaparecido. Una de las excepciones notables a esta desaparición es la publicación en 2005 de la Tesis doctoral del francés Nicolás Rey, *Quand la Révolution, aux Amériques, était Nègre... Caraïbes Noirs, Negros Franceses et autres «Oubliés» de l'Histoire*. En un artículo aparecido en 1976 Nancie González habla justamente de la transformación entre los garífuna de su forma de auto representación, considerando el tránsito de « Caribes negros » a « Garífunas » como un proceso de etnicización que correspondía a transformaciones en los procesos de politización de la identidad influenciada por la experiencia del movimiento indígena pero igualmente del movimiento negro en Estados Unidos. Hay pues una confluencia en el proceso de transformación en los términos de apelación entre los estudios científicos y las autorepresentaciones de estas poblaciones. Esta tendencia se reforzará en los años 1990 con el advenimiento de las políticas de reconocimiento y el papel protagónico que van jugar las poblaciones negras o de origen africano, entre ellas, los garífuna.

Finalmente, a propósito de la distribución por disciplinas realizada por Carlson Tuttle en esta compilación, cerca de la mitad conciernen a la antropología. Si a dichos registros le agregamos las correspondientes a Etnohistoria, Lingüística, Espiritualidad, Música danza y artes, Literatura y Educación y Turismo, más las de Salud y Medicina (que presentan en general una relación entre antropología, ciencias médicas y biológicas), se evidencia el peso de lo cultural en el interés que ha despertado siempre el estudio de estas poblaciones. El resto de referencias, el 10% de la compilación corresponde a trabajos de Historia, muchos de los cuales también presentan conexiones muy fuertes con la cultura. Hay que señalar que igualmente varios trabajos sobre problemáticas contemporáneas podrían clasificarse también como pertenecientes a la sociología o a las ciencias políticas.

De 331 libros registrados 155 (47%) son publicados en los Estados Unidos, mientras que el 53% restante corresponde a publicaciones en América latina (40 %) y Europa (13%). En cuanto a los trabajos universitarios, de 102 referencias registradas en la compilación, hay 65 tesis doctorales y 37 master y licenciaturas. De estos trabajos el 90% han sido realizados en universidades de los Estados Unidos. Para los artículos de revistas y demás referencias (455) se evidencia la predominancia del inglés como lengua de publicación (85%).

En materia de trabajos universitarios es muy fuerte la supremacía de las universidades de los Estados Unidos. Sin embargo, las referencias comienzan gradualmente a diversificarse a partir de los años 1980, en particular con el surgimiento de publicaciones realizadas en los países centroamericanos con población garífuna (principalmente Honduras y Belice).

Esta compilación, a través del tiempo (publicaciones desde el siglo XVII al XXI), de los múltiples espacios geográficos donde han surgido y de la diversidad de formatos permite observar la existencia de una producción bibliográfica importante pero dispersa y parcialmente conocida aun por los especialistas y otros interesados en el tema. Qué no decir de parte del público que se interesa en las poblaciones negras de otras regiones del mundo y que en múltiples casos desconocen hasta la existencia de los garífuna. Es por esto que los programas AFRODESC – EURESCL, fiel a sus objetivos se complace en poder hacer este aporte de edición y difusión del trabajo de Carlson Tuttle. Esta compilación está disponible en formato PDF en el sitio <ird.fr/afrodesc>.

Las personas interesadas en recibirla en forma de base de datos (lo que les permitirá revisar las referencias en orden alfabético de autores, en orden cronológico, por lugar de edición -para libros y tesis-, etc. podrán hacer una solicitud a <ceagarifuna@gmail.com> y se les hará un envío del archivo a la dirección e-mail indicada.

Finalmente, como coordinador de este trabajo de edición no puedo terminar esta presentación sin señalar que el apoyo y participación de Odile Hoffmann, fue determinante para su finalización. Agradezco igualmente a mi hija Mayra Agudelo el trabajo de traducción francés-español-inglés de la presente introducción y la presentación de Carlson Tuttle.

Carlos Agudelo
Sociólogo- Investigador AFRODESC-EURESCL
Investigador asociado URMIS
Unidad de Investigación Migrations et Société
www.unice.fr/urmis/

Anthropology / Anthropologie/ Antropología

Acosta Saignes, Miguel (1950). *Tlacaxipeualiztli, Un Complejo Mesoamericano Entre los Caribes.* Caracas: Instituto de Antropología y Geografía, Facultad de Filosofía y Letras, Universidad Central.

Adams, Richard N. (1956). «Cultural Components of Central America». *American Anthropologist,* 58, 881- 907.

Adams, Sharon Wilcox (2001). *The Garifuna of Belize: Strategies of Representation.* B.A. Honors Thesis, Mary Washington College.

Adams, Sharon Wilcox (2006). *Reconstructing Identity: Re-presentational Strategies in the Garifuna Community of Dangriga, Belize.* M. A. Thesis, University of Texas, Austin.

Agudelo, Carlos (2010). «Génesis de Redes Transnacionales. Movimientos Afrolatinoamericanos en América Central» in Odile Hoffmann (ed.) *Política e Identidad. Afrodescendientes en México y América Central.* México: INAH, UNAM, CEMCA, IRD, pp. 65-92.

Agudelo, Carlos (2011). «Les Garifuna. Transnationalité Territoriale, Construction d'Identités et Action Politique». *REMI, Revue Européenne des Migrations Internationales,* 27 (1), 47-70.

Agudelo, Carlos (2011). «Os Garífunas: Transnacionalidade Territorial, Construção de Identidades et Ação Política». *Desigualdade and Diversidade. Revista de Ciências Sociais da PUC Rio,* 8 (jun/jul), 51-76. <http://publique.rdc.puc-rio.br/desigualdadediversidade/> viewed 6 Decembet 2011.

Agudelo, Carlos (2012). «Qu'est-ce Qui Vient Après la Reconnaissance? Multiculturalisme et Populations Noires en Amérique latine» in Christian Gros et David Dumoulin Kervran (eds.) *Le Multiculturalisme au Concret. Un Modèle Latino Américain?.* Paris: Presses Sorbonne Nouvelle, pp. 267-277.

Agudelo, Carlos (2012). «The Afro-guatemalan Political Mobilization: Between Identity, Construction Process, Global Influences and Institutionalization» in Jean Rahier (ed.) *Black*

Social Movements in Latin America. From Monocultural Mestizaje to Multiculturalism. Miami: Palgrave Macmillan.

Agudelo, Carlos (2012). «Los Garifunas, Identidades y Reivindicaciones de un Pueblo Afrodescendiente de América Central" in CINU-Centro de información de las Naciones Unidas (ed.) *Afrodescendencia: Aproximaciones Contemporáneas desde América Latina y el Caribe,* pp. 59-66. <cinu.mx/ AFRODESCENDENCIA.pdf> viewed 6 April 2012.

Allaire, Louis (1980). «On the Historicity of Carib Migration in the Lesser Antilles». *American Antiquity,* 45 (2), 238-245.

Allaire, Louis (1997). «The Island Caribs of the Lesser Antilles» in Samuel M. Wilson (ed.) *The Indigenous People of the Caribbean.* Gainesville: University Press of Florida, pp. 177-185.

Álvarez Sambulá, Francisco (2008). *Alternabilidad en el Poder como Mecanismo para la Consolidación de la Democracia en Centro América, Factor Básico para la Vigencia del Tratado Marco de Seguridad Democrática.* Tegucigalpa: Centro de Cultura Garífuna.

Amason Montero, Erin (2010). *The Construction of Blackness in Honduran Cultural Production.* Ph.D. Thesis, University of New Mexico.

Amaya Banegas, Jorge Alberto (2004). *'Reimaginando' la Nación en Honduras: de la 'Nación Homogénea' a la 'Nación Pluriétnica'. Los Negros Garífunas de Cristales, Trujillo.* Tesis Doctoral, Universidad Complutense de Madrid.

Amaya, Jorge (2005). «Las Imágenes de los Negros Garífunas en la Literatura Hondureña: La Construcción de Discursividades Nacionales Excluyentes». *Boletín* AFEHC, 13. <http://afe-hchistoriacentroamericana.org/index.php?action=fi_affan-did=378> viewed 6 January 2011.

Amaya, Jorge y Germán Moncada (2002). *La Comunidad Garífuna y sus Desafíos de Cara al Siglo XXI, (1ª edición).* La Ceiba: Organización de Desarrollo Étnico Comunitario (ODECO), PROGRAFIP.

Anderson, A. L. (2002). *Of One Accord: Garifuna Collective Action and the Social Transformation of the Guatemalan Peace*

Process in Labuga (1996--1998). Ph.D. Thesis, University of California, Santa Cruz.

Anderson, Mark (1997). «The Significance of Blackness: Representations of Garifuna in St Vincent and Central America, 1700-1900». *Transforming Anthropology,* 6 (1-2), 22-35.

Anderson, Mark (2000). *Garífuna Kids: Blackness, Modernity, and Tradition in Honduras.* Ph.D. Thesis, University of Texas at Austin.

Anderson, Mark (2001). «Existe el Racismo en Honduras? Discursos Garífunas Sobre Raza y Racismo». *Mesoamerica,* 22 (42), 135-63.

Anderson, Mark and Sarah England (2004). «Autentica Cultura Africana en Honduras? Los Afro-Centroamericanos Desafían el Mestizaje Indo-Hispánico Hondureño» in D. Araque, J. Gould, and C.R. Hale (ed.) *Memorias del Mestizaje: Cultura Política en Centroamérica de 1920 al Presente.* Antigua, Guatemala: Centro de Investigaciones Regionales de Mesoamérica, pp. 253-293.

Anderson, Mark (2005). «Bad Boys and Peaceful Garifuna: Transnational Encounters between Racial Stereotypes of Honduras and the United States» in A. Dzidzienyo and S. Oboler (ed.) *Neither Enemies nor Friends: Latinos. Blacks, Afro-Latinos.* New York: Palgrave Macmillian, pp. 101-116.

Anderson, Mark (2005). «Garifuna Politics and Indigenous Rights in Honduras» presented at 2005 Latin American Studies Annual Meetings.

Anderson, Mark (2007). «When Afro Becomes (like) Indigenous: Garifuna and Afro-Indigenous Politics in Honduras». *Journal of Latin American and Caribbean Anthropology,* 12 (2), 384-413.

Anderson, Mark (2008). «The Complicated Career of Hugh Smythe, Anthropologist and Ambassador: The Early Years, 1940-1950». *Transforming Anthropology,* 16 (2), 128-146.

Anderson, Mark ((2009) Black and Indigenous. Garifuna activism and consumer culture in Honduras, Minneapolis, University of Minnesota Press, p. 290.

Anderson, Mark (2010). «Los Garífuna Hondureños y los Significados de "Negro" en los Años 1930 y 1940» in Elizabeth Cunin (ed.) *Mestizaje, Diferencia y Nación. Lo "Negro" en América Central y el Caribe.* México: INAH, CEMCA, UNAM, IRD, pp. 35-67.

Anderson, Mark (2012). «Garifuna Activism and the Corporatist Honduras State since the 2009 Coup» in Jean Rahier, (ed.). *Black Social Movements in Latin America. From Monocultural Mestizaje to Multiculturalism.* Miami: Palgrave Macmillan.

Armand, Michèle (1984). *Loubavagu ou L'autre Rive Lointaine: Parmi les Théâtres de l'Identité, le Théâtre des Indiens Caraïbes noirs dits Garifunas: Etude Comparative.* Thèse de Doctorat Université Paris VIII.

Arnaud, Gérald (2005). «Garifuna: un Morceau d'Afrique en Amérique». *AFRICULTURES,* 62. <http://www.africultures. com/php/index.php?nav=articleandno=3725> viewed 6 January 2011.

Arrivillaga Cortés, Alfonso (1985). «Etnografía de la Fiesta de San Isidro Labrador. Livingston, Izabal, Guatemala». *La Tradición Popular,* 54, 1-16.

Arrivillaga Cortés, Alfonso (1989). «Expresiones Culturales Garífuna de Guatemala». *Tradición Popular,* 75, 1-13.

Arrivillaga Cortés, Alfonso (1992). «La Estructura Político: Administrativa y sus Implicaciones en el Pueblo Garífuna de Guatemala». *Anales del Caribe,* 12, 211-217.

Arrivillaga Cortés, Alfonso (1998). «Petén y sus Fronteras Culturales: Notas para un Esbozo Histórico Cultural». *Fronteras: Espacios de Encuentros y Transgresiones. Universidad de Costa Rica,* 51-60.

Arrivillaga Cortés, Alfonso (1998). *Los Garinagu y los Acuerdos de Paz: Nota sobre la Niñez y Juventud.* Guatemala: PRONICE.

Arrivillaga Cortés, Alfonso (2004). «Sobre el Idioma Garífuna y Estudios». *Tradiciones de Guatemala,* 61, 18-28.

Arrivillaga Cortés, Alfonso (2007). «Asentamientos Caribes (Garífuna) en Centroamérica: de Héroes Fundadores a

Espíritus Protectores». *Boletín de Antropología, Universidad de Antioquia,* 21 (38), 227-252.

Arrivillaga Cortés, Alfonso (2008). «Els Garífunes en les Fronteres del Golf d'Honduras: Memòria i Territorialitat». *Revista d'Etnologia de Catalunya,* 33, 74-81.

Arrivillaga Cortés, Alfonso (2009). *La Población Garífuna Migrante.* Guatemala: CODISRA.

Arrivillaga Cortés, Alfonso (2009). «Ciudadanías Transnacionales en la Diáspora Garífuna» in Jorge Ramón González Ponciano y Miguel Lisbona (ed.) *México y Guatemala: Entre el Liberalismo y la Democracia Multicultural -azares de una transición política inconclusa-.* México: IIF-IIA-UNAM, pp. 193-210.

Arrivillaga Cortés, Alfonso (2010). «La diáspora garífuna entre memorias y fronteras». *Boletín de Antropología Universidad de Antioquia,* 24 (41), 84-95.

Arrivillaga Cortés, Alfonso and Sylvia Shaw A. (1997). «Recomendaciones de Lecturas sobre los Garífuna». *Estudios - Instituto de Investigaciones Históricas, Antropológicas y Arqueológicas, Guatemala,* 2 (August), 74-83.

Arrivillaga, Alfonso y Alfredo Gómez (1988). «Antecedentes históricos, movilizaciones sociales y reivindicaciones étnicas en la cota atlántica de Guatemala». *Estudios Sociales Centroamericanos,* 48, 35-48. <http://aprendeenlinea. udea.edu.co/revistas/index.php/boletin/article/view-File/7945/7447> viewed 6 January 2011.

Avila, Tomas Alberto and José Francisco Avila (eds.) (2008). *Garifuna World.* Providence: Milenio Associates, LLC.

Baker, Patrick (1988). «Ethnogenesis: The Case of the Dominica Caribs». *America Indigena,* 48 (2), 377-401.

Baker, Patrick (1994). *Centring the Periphery: Chaos, Order, and the Ethnohistory of Dominica.* Montreal and Kingston: McGill-Queen's University Press.

Ballet, J. (1875). «Les Caraibes». *International Congres des Americanistes,* 1, 398-438.

Banks, E.P. (1954). *An Inquiry into the Structure of Island Carib Culture.* Ph.D. Thesis, Harvard University.

Banks, E.P. (1955). «Island Carib Folk Tales». *Caribbean Quarterly,* 4 (1), 32-39.

Banks, E.P. (1956). «A Carib Village in Dominica». *Social and Economic Studies,* 5 (1), 74-86.

Bass, J. O. Jobe Jr (1999). *Garifuna Seashore, Creole Riverside: an Ethnogeographic Investigation of Two Belizean Villages.* M.A. Thesis, Louisiana State University.

Basso, Ellen B. (ed.) (1977). *Carib-Speaking Indians, Culture, Society and Language.* Tucson: University of Arizona Press.

Bastide, Roger (1971). *African Civilisations in the New World.* New York: Harper and Row, p. 232.

Bastide, Roger (1996). *Les Amériques Noires.* Paris: L'Harmattan.

Beaucage, Pierre (1966). «Les Caraïbes Noirs: Trois Siècles de Changement Social». *Anthropologica,* 8 (2), 175-195.

Beaucage, Pierre (1970). *Economic Anthropology of the Black Carib of Honduras.* Ph.D. Thesis, University of London.

Beaucage, Pierre (1982). «Echanges, Inequalites, Guerre: La Cas des Caraïbes Insulaires (XVIIe et XVIIIe Siècles.)». *Recherches Amerindiennes au Quebec,* 12 (3), 179-191.

Beaucage, Pierre (1988). «L'Ancêtre et le Maitre des Poissons; Notes sur un Mythe d'Origine du Chamanisme chez les Garifona du Honduras». *Recherches Amerindiennes au Quebec,* 18 (2-3), 83-90.

Beaucage, Pierre (1989). «L'effort et la Vie: Ethnosemantique du Travail chez les Garifonas du Honduras et les Maseuals (Nahuats) du Mexique». *Labour, Capital and Society,* 22 (1), 111-137.

Beaucage, Pierre (1995). «Donner et Prendre. Garifunas et Yanomamis». *Anthropologie et Sociétés,* 19 (1-2), 95-117.

Beaucage, Pierre (2007). «Entre la Mer et la Forêt: La Gestion des Ressources Végétales par les Garifunas du Nord-Est du Honduras au Milieu du XXe Siècle». *Recherches Amérindiennes au Québec,* 36 (1), 81-94.

Bonner, Donna Maria (1999). *Garifuna Town/ Caribbean Nation/ Latin American State: Identity and Prejudice in Belize*. Ph.D. Thesis, University of New York at Buffalo.

Borgia, Vito (1958). *Contributo allo Studio di Dermatoglifi di» Caribi Neri» del Honduras Britanico*. Ph.D. Thesis, Palermo University.

Borgia, Vito (1976). «A Dermatoglyphic Study of the Black Caribs of British Honduras». *Actes du XLIIe Congres International des Americanistes*, 6, 525-534.

Brigham, William T. (1887). *Guatemala: The Land of the Quetzal*. New York: Charles Scribner's Sons.

Brondo, Keri (2006). *Roots, Rights, and Belonging: Garifuna Indigeneity and Land Rights on Honduras' North Coast*. Ph.D. Thesis, Michigan State University.

Brondo, Keri (2007). «Land Loss and Garifuna Women's Activism on Honduras' North Coast». *Journal of International Women's Studies*, 9 (1), 99-116.

Brondo, Keri Vacanti (2010). «When Mestizo Becomes (Like) Indio, or Is It Garífuna?: Multicultural Rights and "Making Place" on Honduras' North Coast». *The Journal of Latin American and Caribbean Anthropology*, 15 (1), 170-194.

Broomfield, Padmini and Cynara Davies (2003). «Costeño Voices: Oral History on Nicaragua's Caribbean Coast». *Oral History*, 31 (1), 85-94.

Brown, Edward A., M. Ogaldez and Una Mae Gordon (1980). *The Belizean Garifuna*. Dangriga: Dangriga Education Committee.

Bullard, M. Kenyon (1974). «Hide and Secrete: Woman's Sexual Magic in Belize». *The Journal of Sex Research*, 10 (4), 259-265.

Buttram, Mance Edwin (2007). *Completing the Circle: Garifuna Pilgrimage Journeys from Belize to Yurumein (St. Vincent and the Grenadines)*. M.A. Thesis, University of Arizona.

Byard, P. J. and F. C. Lee (1982). «Colorimetry in Belize, II, Inter- and Intra-Population Variation». *American Journal of Physical Anthropology*, 58 (2), 215-219.

Campbell, Joseph (1989). *Historical Atlas of World Mythology Vol. II: The Way of the Seeded Earth Part 3: Mythologies of the Primitive Planters: The Middle and Southern America.* New York: Harper and Row.

Cayetano, Marion and Roy Cayetano (2005). «Garífuna Language, Dance, and Music: A Masterpiece of the Oral and Intangible Heritage of Humanity. How Did it Happen?» in Joseph O. Palacio (ed.) *The Garífuna, a Nation Across Borders: Essays in Social Anthropology.* Belize: Cubola Books, pp. 230–250.

Cayetano, Phyllis (2003). «Indigenous Land Rights, Development and Environment: a Garifuna Perspective» presented at The Indigenous Rights in the Commonwealth: Caribbean and Americas Regional Expert Meeting, 23-25 June. <cpsu.org.uk/downloads/Phyllis_Cayetano.pdf> viewed 6 January 2011.

Chala Santiago, Valencia (1986). *El Negro en Centroamerica.* Quito, Ecuador: Centro Cuntural Afro-Ecuatoriano, Abya-Yala.

Chernela, Janet M. (1991). «Symbolic Inaction in Rituals of Gender and Procreation among the Garifuna (Black Caribs) of Honduras». *Ethos,* 19 (1), 52-67.

Coehlo, Ruy Galvao de Andrade (1955). *The Black Carib of Honduras.* Ph.D. Thesis, Northwestern University.

Coehlo, Ruy Galvao de Andrade (1964). «Os Karaib Negros de Honduras». *Revista do Museu Paulista, N. S.,* XV, 4-212.

Coehlo, Ruy Galvao de Andrade (1995). *Los Negros Caribes de Honduras.* Tegucigalpa: Editorial Guaymuras.

Coelho, Ruy Galvao de Andrade (1949). «The Significance of the Couvade among the Black Carib». *Man,* 49 (63,64), 51-53.

Coelho, Ruy Galvao de Andrade (1952). «Le Concept de L'ame Chez les Caraïbes Noirs». *Journal de la Société des Américanistes,* 41 (1), 21-30.

Coelho, Ruy Galvao de Andrade (1953). «As Festas dos Caribes Negros». *Anhembi,* 26, 55-72.

Cohen, Jon (2006). «Honduras: Why So High? A Knotty Story». *Science,* 313 (5786), 481-483.

Comitas, Lambros (1968). *Caribbeana 1900-1965, A Topical Bibliography.* Seattle: University of Washington Press.

Conzemius, Eduard (1928). «Ethnographic Notes on the Black Carib (Garif)». *American Anthropologist,* 30 (2), 183-205.

Conzemius, Eduard (1930). «Sur les Garif ou Caraïbes Noirs de l'Amerique». *Anthropos,* 25, 859-877.

Cooper, Vincent O. (1997). «Language and Gender among the Kalinago of Fifteenth-century St. Croix» in Samuel M. Wilson (ed.) *The Indigenous People of the Caribbean.* Gainesville: University Press of Florida, pp. 186-196.

Cosminsky, Sheila and Emory Whipple (1984). «Ethnicity and Mating Patterns in Punta Gorda, Belize» in Michael H. Crawford (ed.) *Current Developments in Anthropological Genetics. Vol. 3: Black Caribs: A Case Study in Biocultural Adaptation.* New York: Plenum Press, pp. 115-132.

Cosminsky, Sheila (1976). «Carib-Creole Relations in a Belizean Community» in Mary W. Helms and Franklin O. Loveland (eds.) *Frontier Adaptations in Lower Central America.* Philadelphia: Institute for the Study of Human Issues, pp. 95-114.

Cosminsky, Sheila (1977). «Interethnic Relations in a Southern Belizean Community». *Ethnicity,* 4, 226-245.

Cosminsky, Shelia and Mary Scrimshaw (1982). «Sex Roles and Subsistence: A Comparative Analysis of Three Central American Communities» in Christine A. Loveland and Franklin O. Loveland (eds.) *Sex Roles and Social Change in Native Lower Central American Societies.* Urbana: University of Illinois, pp. 44-69.

Craft, Linda J. (1998). «Ethnicity, Oral Tradition, and the Processed Word: Construction of a National Identity in Honduras». *Revista Hispánica Moderna,* 51 (1), 136-146.

Craven, Catherine Elisabeth (2009). *We Are Not Just the Future, We Are the Present. Exploring the Developmental Needs of Young*

Garifunas in Rural and Urban Honduras. M.A. Thesis, Simon Frazer University.

Crawford, Michael H, (1984). «Problems and Hypotheses: An Introduction» in Michael H. Crawford (ed.) *Current Developments in Anthropological Genetics. Vol. 3: Black Caribs: A Case Study in Biocultural Adaptation.* New York: Plenum Press, pp. 1-9.

Crawford, Michael H. (1983). «The Anthropological Genetics of the Black Caribs (Garifuna) of Central America and the Caribbean». *Yearbook of Physical Anthropology,* 26, 161-192.

Crawford, Michael H. (ed.) (1984). *Current Developments in Anthropological Genetics. Vol. 3: Black Caribs: A Case Study in Biocultural Adaptation.* New York: Plenum Press.

Crawford, Michael H. and Nancie L. González. (1981). «The Black Caribs (Garifuna) of Livingston, Guatemala: Genetic Markers and Admixture Estimates". *Human Biology,* 53, 87-103.

Cunin, Elisabeth and Odile Hoffmann (coords.) (2009). *Etnicidad y Nacion: Debate Alrededor do Belice, Belize: Ethnicity and Nation.* Mexico City: AFRODESC, Working Paper No. 5.

Custodio, R. (1984). «Blood Groups, Haemoglobin, and Plasma Proteinpolymorphisms in Black Carib Populations» in Michael H. Crawford (ed.) *Current Developments in Anthropological Genetics. Vol. 3: Black Caribs: A Case Study in Biocultural Adaptation.* New York: Plenum Press, pp. 289-301.

Davidas, Lionel (1998). «The Dominican Karifuna Indians' Fight for Survival». *Dialectical Anthropology,* 23 (4), 415-24.

Davidson, William V. (1974). «The Caribs (Garífuna) of Central America. A Map of their Realm and Bibliography of Research». *National Studies,* 2 (6), 15-25.

Davidson, William V. (1979). «The Garifuna Symposium: An Introduction». *Actes du XLIIe Congres International de Americanistes,* 6, 447-450.

Davidson, William V. (1982). « In Search of Garifuna, Beachfolk of the Bay of Honduras». *National Geographic Society Research Reports,* 14, 129-141.

Davidson, William V. (1984). «El Padre Subirana y las Tierras Concedidas a los Indios Hondurenos en el Siglo XIX». *America Indigena*, XLIV (3), 447-459.

Davidson, William V. (1984). «The Garifuna in Central America: Ethnohistorical and Geographical Foundations» in Michael H. Crawford (ed.) *Current Developments in Anthropological Genetics. Vol. 3: Black Caribs: A Case Study in Biocultural Adaptation.* New York: Plenum Press, pp. 13-35.

Davidson, William V. (1987). «The Amerindians of Belize, an Overview». *America Indigena*, XLVII (1), 9-22.

Davis, Dave D. and R. Christopher Goodwin (1990). «Island Carib Origins: Evidence and Nonevidence». *American Antiquity*, 55 (1), 37-48.

de la Paix, Armand (1929). «Relation de l'Isle de la Guadeloupe» in Joseph Rennard (ed.) *Les Caraibes, La Guadeloupe: 1635-1656.* Paris: Librairie générale et internationale G.Fieker, pp 23-127.

DeFay, Jason (2004). *Identity Matters: Immigration and the Social Construction of Identity in Garifuna in Los Angeles.* Ph.D. Thesis, University of California, San Diego.

Delawarde, R.P. J.-B. (1938). «Les Derniers Caraibes: Leur Vie dans une Reserve de la Dominique». *Journal de la Societe des Americanistes de Pari*, 30, 167-204.

Demazière, Eve (1994). *Les Cultures Noires d'Amérique Centrale.* París: Karthala.

Demiciriyan, Vanessa (2006), *A la Recherché d'un Peuple: les Caribes noirs de Saint Vincent, leurs Descendants et leur Diaspora*, Master 1, Université Paris 8.

Demiciriyan, Vanessa (2007), *Essai d'Anthropologie des Garifunas de Saint Vincent*, Master 2 Université Paris I IEDES.

Devor, E. and Crawford, M. H. and Bach-Enciso, V. (1984). «Genetic Population Structure of the Black Caribs and Creoles» in Michael H. Crawford (ed.) *Current Developments in Anthropological Genetics. Vol. 3: Black Caribs: A Case Study in Biocultural Adaptation.* New York: Plenum Press, pp. 365-379.

Dewey, Eliza Morgan (2010). *An Opportunity to Identify Ourselves»: Garifuna Poltical Affiliation in the Nicaraquan Civil*

War, 1980-1990. Thesis (A.B., Honors in Social Studies) Harvard University.

Diego, Judy (1979). *Garifuna Clothing*. Belize: self published.

Dreyfus, Simone (1976). «Territoire et Residence Chez les Caraibes Insulaires au XVII Siecle». *International Congress of Amerianiste*, 2, 35-46.

Drusine, Helen (2005). «The Garifuna Fight Back». *Third Text*, 19 (2), 197-202.

Eaden, John (ed., transl. and abridged by 1970). *1931 Memoirs of Pere Labat*. London: Frank Cass and Co.

Elington Lambi, Gerardo (1998). *Derecho Consuetudinario Garífuna sobre la Posesión y el Uso de las Playas en el Perímetro Urbano del Municipio de Livingston, Departamento de Izabal*. Tesis (Abogado y Notario), Universidad de San Carlos de Guatemala.

Ellington Lambi, Geraldo (1988). «Ladairagun Garifuna Lungua. Ubicacion y Situacion Actual de la Garifuna de Guatemala». *Estudios - Instituto de Investigaciones Históricas, Antropológicas y Arqueológicas*, 2, 45-51.

England, Sarah and Mark Anderson (1998). «Authentic African Culture in Honduras? Afro-Central Americans Challenge Honduran Indo-HispanicMestizaje» prepared for presentation at the XXI Latin American Studies Association International Congress, September 24-27, Chicago, <http://168.96.200.17/ar/libros/lasa98/England-Anderson.pdf> viewed 6 January 2011.

England, Sarah (1994). «No Life without Land, Interview with Teofilo Lacayo». *Abya Yala News. Oakland*, 8 (2), 24.

England, Sarah (1998). «Gender Ideologies and Domestic Structures within the Transnational Space of the Garifuna Diaspora» in C.A. Moreland (ed.) *Diasporic Identity: Selected Papers on Refugees and Immigrants Vol. VI*. Arlington: American Anthropological Association, pp. 133-57.

England, Sarah (1999). «Negotiating Race and Place in the Garifuna Diaspora: Identity Formation and Transnational

Grassroots Politics in New York City and Honduras». *Identities*, 6 (1), 5-54.

England, Sarah (2000). *Creating a Global Garífuna Nation. The Transnationalization of Race, Class, Gender and Politics in the Garífuna Diaspora*. Ph.D. Thesis, University of California, Davis.

England, Sarah (2006). *Afro-Central Americans in New York City: Garifuna Tales of Transnational Movements in Racialized Space*. Gainesville: University of Florida Press.

England, Sarah (2010). «Mixed and Multiracial in Trinidad and Honduras: Rethinking Mixed-race Identities» in Latin America and the Caribbean». *Ethnic and Racial Studies*, 33 (2), 195-213.

Euraque, Dario (2002). «Negros y Mulatos en la Evangelización y Civilización de los Pueblos Indígenas de Honduras, ca. 1750-1860» Ponencia al VI Congreso Centroamericano de Historia, Panamá.

Euraque, Dario (2003). «200 Años de Categorías Raciales y Etnicas en Honduras, 1790-1990s» presented at Tercera Conferencia Internacional, Población del istmo centroamericano», San José, (Costa Rica).

Euraque, Dario (2003). «The Threat of Blackness to the Mestizo Nation: Race and Ethnicity in the Honduran Banana Economy, 1920's and 1930's» in S. Striffler and M. Moberg (eds.) *Banana Wars: Power, Production, and History in the Americas*. Durham: Duke University Press, pp. 229-252.

Firschein, I. Lester (1961). «Population Dynamics of the Sickle-Cell trait in the Black Caribs of British Honduras, Central America». *American Journal of Human Genetics*, 13 (2), 233-254.

Firschein, I. Lester (1984). «Demographic Patterns of the Garifuna (Black Caribs) of Belize» in Michael H. Crawford (ed.) *Black Caribs: A Case Study of Biocultural Adaptation. Current Developments in Anthropological Genetics. Vol. 3*. New York: Plenum Press, pp. 67-93.

Fleming, Ilah (1972). «Guatemala». *Guatemala Indigena*, 7 (4), 141-152.

Forte, Maximilian C. (1990). «Renewed Indigeneity in the Local-Global Continuum and the Political Economy of Tradition: The Case of Trinidad's Caribs and The Caribbean Organization of Indigenous People» <http://www.centrelink.org/renewed.html> viewed 4 April 2011.

Forte, Maximilian C. (2002). «Our Amerindian Ancestors: The State, the Nation, and the Revaluing of Indigeneity in Trinidad and Tobago». *Issues in Caribbean Amerindian Studies,* <http://www.centrelink.org/Forte.html> viewed 3 April 2011.

Forte, Maximilian C. (2004). «Writing the Caribs Out: The Construction and Demystification of the 'Deserted Island' Thesis for Trinidad». Issues in Caribbean Amerindian Studies, 6 (3) <http://www.centrelink.org/forteatlantic2004.pdf> viewed 6 January 2011.

Forte, Maximilian C. (2005). «Extinction: The Historical Trope of Anti-Indigeneity in the Caribbean». *Issues in Caribbean Amerindian Studies,* 6 (4) <http://www.centrelinkh.org/forteatlantic2005.pdf> viewed 3 April 2011.

Forte, Maximilian C. (2006). *Indigenous Resurgence in the Contemporary Caribbean.* New York: Peter Lang.

Foster, Bayron (2005). «Aspects of Garifuna Male Female Relations» in Joseph O. Palacio (ed.), *The Garifuna: A Nation across Borders: Essays in Social Anthropology.* Belice: Editorial Cubola, pp.123-136.

Foster, Bayron (2005). «Heart Drum: Spirit Possession in the Garifuna communities of Belize» in Joseph O. Palacio (ed.), *The Garifuna: A Nation across Borders: Essays in Social Anthropology.* Belice: Editorial Cubola, pp.159-175.

Foster, Byron (1988). «Estructura Familiar Garifuna». *América Indigena,* 48 (2), 233-283.

Franzone, Dorothy Lawrence (1994). *A Critical and Cultural Analysis of an African People in the Americas: Africanisms in the Garifuna Culture in Belize.* Ph.D. Thesis, Temple University.

Gale, Rivera and Lorena Araceli (2001). *Características Generales de los Garífunas Conforme a los Resultados del XI Censo Nacional y V de Vivienda Año 2001.* Tegucigalpa: Instituto Nacional de Estadística.

Gallardo, Mario (2007). *La Danta que Hizo Dugú: Literatura Oral en la Comunidad Garífuna de Masca.* Tegucigalpa: Secretaría de Cultura, Artes y Deportes.

Gallardo, Mario (2007). «La Persistencia de la Memoria: Tradición Oral de los Garífunas de la Costa Atlántica de Honduras». Especulo: Revista de Estudios Literarios, 35 <http://www.ucm.es/info/especulo/numero35/garifun.html> viewed 4 April 2011.

Gargallo, Francesa (2005). «Garifuna: A Culture of Women and Men» in Joseph O. Palacio (ed.) *The Garifuna, A Nation Across Borders: Essays in Social Anthropology.* Belize: Cubola Books, pp. 137-158.

Gargallo, Francesca (1992). «Los Afroindoamericanos de Belice: La Cultura Garifuna». *Cuadernos Americanos,* 1 (31), 159-170.

Gargallo, Francesca (1999). «El Pueblo Garífuna: Caribes y Cimarrones Hoy». *Cuadernos Americanos,* 4 (76), 109-149.

Gargallo, Francesca (2000). «Los Garífuna de Centroamérica: Reubicación, Sobrevivencia y Nacionalidad de un Pueblo Afroindoamericano». *Politica y Cultura,* 14, 89-107.

Gargallo, Francesca (2002). *Garífuna, Garínagu, Caribe: Historia de una Nacion Libertaria.* México: Siglo XXI Editores.

Gauvain, Mary and Robert L Munroe (2009). «Mixed and Multiracial in Trinidad and Honduras: Rethinking Mixed-race Identities in Latin America and the Caribbean». *Child Development,* 80 (6), 16-28.

Ghidinelli, Azzo and Massajoli, Pieleone (1984). «Resumen Etnografico de los Caribes Negros (Garifunas) de Honduras». *America Indigena,* 44 (3), 485-518.

Ghidinelli, Azzo (1972). «Aspectos Economicos de la Cultura de los Caribes Negros del Municipio de Livingston». *Guatemala Indigena,* 7 (4), 71-141.

Ghidinelli, Azzo (1972). «I Reporti Economici Interetnici a Livingston». *Terra America,* 8 (28), 13-31.

41

Ghidinelli, Azzo (1975). «Apuntes para una Teoria y una Metodologia de la Investigacion sobre el Roce Interetnico». *Guatemala Indigena*, 10 (1-2), 3-212.

Ghidinelli, Azzo (1976). «La Familia entre los Caribes Negros, Ladinos y Kekchies de Livingston». *Guatemala Indigena*, 11 (3-4), 4-315.

Ghidinelli, Azzo (1983). «Los Grupos Humanos que se Originaron despues de la Conquista en la Costa Atlantica de Guatemala y Honduras» San Jose, Costa Rica Memoria del Seminario Costa Atlantica de C. America, CSUCA.

Ghidinelli, Azzo (2001). «Etnopsicologia, Etnopschiatria, Etnomedicina: Un Approccio Antropologico per l'Integrazionedi Sistemi Socio-Sanitari». *Revista Scientifica di Psicologia*, (December), 62-75.

Goett, Jennifer Allan (1997). *Waste and Resource: Two Garifuna Households on the North Coast of Honduras.* M.A. Thesis, University of Texas at Austin.

Goett, Jennifer Allan (2006). *Diasporic Identities, Autochthonous Rights: Race, Gender, and the Cultural Politics of Creole Land Rights in Nicaragua.* Ph.D. Thesis, University of Texas, Austin.

González, Nancie L. (1959). «The Nonunilineal Descent Group in the Caribbean and Central America». *American Anthropologist*, 61, 578-583.

González, Nancie L. (1961). «Family Organization in Five Types of Migratory Wage Labor». *American Anthropologist*, 63, 1264-1280.

González, Nancie L. (1963). «Patterns of Diet, Health and Sickness in a Black Carib Community». *Tropical and Geographical Medicine*, 15, 422-430.

González, Nancie L. (1965). «Black Carib Adaptation to a Latin Urban Milieu». *Social and Economic Studies*, 14, 272-277.

González, Nancie L. (1966). «Health Behavior in Cross-cultural Perspective». *Human Organization*, 25, 122-125.

González, Nancie L, (1969). *Black Carib Household Structure: A Study of Migration and Modernization.* Seattle: University of Washington Press.

González, Nancie L, (1970). «The Neoteric Society». *Comparative Studies in Society and History*, 12 (1), 1-13.

González, Nancie L. (1970). «Cachiqueles and Caribs: The Social Context of Field Work» in Freilich, Morris (ed.) *Marginal Natives: Anthropologists at Work*. New York: Harper and Row, pp. 153-184.

González, Nancie L. (1970). «Toward a Definition of Matrifocality» in Norman Whitten, Jr. and John Szwed (eds.) *Afro-American Anthropology: Problems in Theory and Method.* New York: Free Press, pp. 231-243.

González, Nancie L. (1970). «Two Views of Obeah and Witchcraft, 1. Obeah and other Witchcraft among the Black Caribs» in Deward E. Walker Jr. (ed.) *Systems of North American Witchcraft and Sorcery.* Moscow, Idaho: Anthropological Monographs of the University of Idaho, No. 1, pp. 95-108.

González, Nancie L. (1976). «From Black Carib to Garifuna:The Coming of Age of an Ethnic Group». *Actes du XLIIe Congres International des Americanistes*, 6, 577-588.

González, Nancie L. (1979). «Garifuna Settlement in New York: A New Frontier». *International Migration Review*, 13 (2), 255-263.

González, Nancie L. (1979). «Sex Preference in Human Figure Drawings by Garifuna (Black Carib) Children». *Ethnology*, 18 (4), 355-64.

González, Nancie L. (1983). «Changing Sex Roles among the Garifuna (Black Carib) and their Implications for the Family». *Journal of Comparative Family Studies*, 14 (2), 203-213.

González, Nancie L, (1983). «New Evidence on the Origins of the Black Carib». *New West Indian Guide*, 57 (3-4), 143-172.

González, Nancie L, (1984). «The Anthropologist as Female Head of Household». *Feminist Studies*, 10 (1), 97-114.

González, Nancie L. (1984). «Garifuna (Black Carib) Social Organization» in Michael H. Crawford (ed.) *Current Developments in Anthropological Genetics. Vol. 3: Black Caribs: A Case Study in Biocultural Adaptation*. New York: Plenum Press, pp. 51-65.

González, Nancie L. (1984). «Rethinking the Consanguineal Household and Matrifocality». *Ethnology,* 23 (1), 1-12.

González, Nancie L. (1986). «Giving Birth in America: The Immigrant's Dilemma» in Rita J. Simon and Carloine B. Brettell (ed.) *International Immigration: The Female Experience.* Totowa, N.J.: Rowman and Allanheld, pp. 241-253.

González, Nancie L. (1986). «Nueva Evidencia sobre el Origen de los Caribes Negros, con Consideraciones sobre el Significado de la Tradicion». *Mesoamerica,* 12, 331-356.

González, Nancie L. (1987). «Una Mayor Recompensa en el Cielo Actividades de Misioneros Metodistas entre los Amerindios de Belice». *America Indigena,* 47 (1), 139-168.

González, Nancie L. (1988). «Rumbo a Roatan» in Elizabeth de Von Hidelbrand (ed.) *Identidad y Transformacion de las Americas.* Bogotá: 45o. Congreso Internacional de Americanistas, pp. 262-273.

González, Nancie L. (1989). *La Historia del Pueblo Garifuna (Pasado y Presente).* Tegucigalpa: ASEPADE.

González, Nancie L, (1992). «Identitidad Etnica y Artificio en los Encuentros Interetnicos del Caribe» in M. Gutierrez Estevez, M. Leon-Portilla, G.H. Gossen, and J.J. Klor de Alva (eds.) *De Palabra y Obra en el Nuevo Mundo, Vol. 2, Encuentros Interetnicos.* Madrid: Siglo Vientiuno Editores, pp. 403-27.

González, Nancie L. (1992). *Prospero, Caliban and Black Sambo: Colonial Views of the Other in the Caribbean.* College Park: Working Paper No. 11, Lecture Series Department of Spanish and Portuguese, University of Maryland.

González, Nancie L. (1995). «African-derived Religious Behavior in the Caribbean and New York» in Michael W. Coy and Leonard Plotnicov (ed.) *African and African-American Sensibility.* Pittsburgh: University of Pittsburgh Ethnology Monographs, 15, pp. 21-34.

González, Nancie L. (1997). «Garifuna Settlement in New York: A New Frontier» in Constance R. Sutton and Elsa M. Chaney (ed.) *Caribbean Life in New York City: Sociocultural*

Dimensions. New York: The Center for Migration Studies, Inc, pp. 150-159.

González, Nancie L, (1999). «The Garifuna of Central America» in Samuel M. Wilson (ed.) *The Indigenous People of the Caribbean.* Gainesville: University of Florida Press, pp. 197-205.

González, Nancie and Gloria Castillo (2003). «Garifuna» in Carol Ember (ed.), *Encyclopedia of Medical Anthropology: Health & Illness in the World's Cultures,* 2, 672-80.

González, Nancie L. and Charles D. Cheek (1988). «Patron de Asentamiento de los Caribes Negros a Principios del Siglo XIX en Honduras: La Busqueda de un Modo de Vida». *Yaxkin,* 11 (2), 89-108.

González, Nancie L. and Ian Gonzalez (1979). «Five Generations of Garifuna Migration: The Final Chapter». *Migration Today,* 7 (5), 18-20.

Gordon, Edmund T and Galio C Gurdian, Charles R Hale (2003). «Rights, Resources, and the Social Memory of Struggle: Reflections on a Study of Indigenous and Black Community Land Rights on Nicaragua's Atlantic Coast». *Human Organization,* 62 (4), 369-381.

Gordon, Edmund T. and Mark Anderson (1999). «The African Diaspora: Toward an Ethnography of Diasporic Identification». *Journal of American Folklore,* 112 (445), 282-296.

Gordon, Edmund T. (1998). *Disparate Diasporas: Identity and Politics in an African Nicaraguan Community.* Austin: University of Texas Press.

Gorres, Shannon (2009). *Garifuna Place-Making: Hope for the Guatemalan Nation.* M.A. Thesis, University of Kansas.

Gorsuch, Richard L. and M. Louise Barnes (1973). «Stages of Ethical Reasoning and Moral Norms of Carib Youths». *Journal of Cross-Cultural Psychology,* 4 (3), 283-301.

Grizzle Huling, Patricia Kaye (2004). *Unbecoming Black: The Case of the Garifuna.* Ph.D. Thesis, Claremont Graduate University.

Gullick, Charles J.M.R.C. (1969). *The Changing Society of Black Caribs*. B. Litt. Thesis, Oxford University.

Gullick, Charles J.M.R.C. (1974). *Tradition and Change amongst the Caribs of St. Vincent*. Ph.D. Thesis, Oxford University.

Gullick, Charles J.M.R.C. (1976). *Exiled from St. Vincent: The Development of Black Carib Culture in Central America*. Malta: Progress Press.

Gullick, Charles J.M.R.C. (1976). «Carib Ethnicity in a Semi-plural Society». *New Community*, 5 (3), 250-258+N293.

Gullick, Charles J.M.R.C. (1976). «Piaye and Pia Manadi». *Belizean Studies*, 4 (6), 7-12.

Gullick, Charles J.M.R.C. (1976). «The Black Caribs in St. Vincent: The Carib War and Aftermath». *Actes du XLIIe Congres International des Americanistes*, 6, 451-465.

Gullick, Charles J.M.R.C. (1978). «The Ecological Background to the Carib Wars». *Journal of Belizean Affairs*, 6, 51-61.

Gullick, Charles J.M.R.C. (1979). «Ethnic Interaction and Carib Language». *Journal of Belizian Affairs*, 9, 3-20.

Gullick, Charles J.M.R.C. (1980). «Island Carib traditions about their arrival in the Lesser Antilles». *Proceedings of the Eighth International Congress for the Study of the pre-Columbian Cultures of the Lesser Antilles. Anthropological Research Papers* 22, , 464-472.

Gulllick, Charles J.M.R.C. (1984). «The Changing Vincentian Carib Population» in Michael H. Crawford (ed.) *Current Developments in Anthropological Genetics. Vol. 3: Black Caribs: A Case Study in Biocultural Adaptation*. New York: Plenum Press, pp. 37-50.

Gullick, Charles J.M.R.C. (1985). *Myths of a Minority: The Changing Traditions of the Vincentian Caribs*. Assen: Van Gorcum.

Gullick, Charles J.M.R.C. (1994). «Afro-America Religious Mindsets». *Bulletin of Latin American Research*, 13 (3), 319-326.

Gullick, Charles J.M.R.C. (1995). «Communicating Caribness» in Neil L. Whitehead (ed.) *Wolves from the Sea*. Leiden: KITLV Press, pp. 157-170.

Gullick, M.I. (1980). «Changing Carib Cookery». *International Congress for the Study of Pre-Columbian Cultures of the Lesser Antilles*, 8, 481-87.

Gutierrez, Alfredo (1984). *Manual Educativo Cultural Garifuna*. Tegucigalpa: ASEPADE.

Hadel, Richard (1976). «Changing Attitudes Toward the Caribs of Belize». *Actes du XLIIe Congres International des Americanistes*, 6, 561-570.

Hasemann, George (1991). *La Etnologia y la Linguistica en Honduras: Una Mirada Retrospectiva*. Tegucigalpa: Instituto Hondureno de Antropologia e Historia.

Hawtayne, G.H. (1886). «Remarks on the Caribs». *Journal of the Anthropological Institute of Great Britain and Ireland*, 16, 196-199.

Helbig, Karl (1959). *Die Landschaften von Nordost-Honduras, auf Grund Einer Geographischen Studienreise im Jahre 1953*. Gotha: H.Haack. Geographesch-Kartoggraphische Anstalt.

Helms, Mary and Franklin O. Loveland (eds.) (1976). *Frontier Adaptations in Lower Central America*. Philadelphia: Institute for the Study of Human Issues.

Helms, Mary (1969). «The Cultural Ecology of a Colonial Tribe». *Ethnology*, 8, 76-84.

Helms, Mary (1981). «Black Carib Domestic Organzation in Historical Perspective: Traditional Orgins of Contemporary Patterns». *Ethnology*, 20 (1), 77-86.

Henderson, Victoria L. (2008). *Sound As a Dollar? The Propertization of Spectrum Resources and Implications for Non-Profit Community Radio in Guatemala*. M.A. Thesis, Queen's University.

Hernandez, Gilbert Henry (1998). *The Garinagu in the Caribbean Basin: Black Caribs*. Dangriga: F.I. Hernandez Productions.

Herranz, Atanacio (1992). *Politica del Lenguaje en Honduras: 1502-1991*. Tesis de Doctorado en Filologia Romanica, Universidad Complutense de Madrid.

Herranz, Atanacio (1996). *Estado, Sociedad y Lenguaje. La Política Lingüística en Honduras*. Tegucigalpa: Editorial Guaymuras.

Hodge, Walter H. (1942). «Plants Used by the Dominica Caribs». *Journal of the New York Botanical Garden*, 43 (512), 189-201.

Hodge, Walter H. and Douglas M. Taylor (1957). «Ethnobotany of the Island Caribs of Dominica». *Webbia*, 12 (2), 513-644.

Hofman, Corinne L. and Alistair J. Bright, Arie Boomert, and Sebastiaan Knippenberg (2007). «Island Rhythms: The Web of Social Relationships and Interaction Networks in the Lesser Antillean Archipelago between 400 B.C. and A.D. 1492». *Latin American Antiquity*, 18 (3), 243-268.

Holdren, Ann Cody (1998). *Raiders and Traders: Caraibe Social and Political Networks at the Time of European Contact and Colonization in the Eastern Caribbean*. Ph.D. Thesis, University of California, Los Angeles.

Honychurch, Lennox (1995). *The Dominica Story, A History of the Island*. London: Macmillan Caribbean.

Honychurch, Lennox (2003). «Chatoyer's Artist: Agostino Brunias and the Depiction of St Vincent» <http://www.lennoxhonychurch.com/article.cfm?id=352> viewed 3 February 2011.

Howland, Lillian G. (1981). «Communicational Intergration of Reality and Fiction». *Language and Communication*, 1 (2), 89-148.

Howland, Michael C. (1980). «Ethnicity and Economic Intergration in Southern Belize». *Ethnicity*, 7 (2), 121-136.

Hulme, Peter (1986). *Colonial Encounters: Europe and the Native Caribbean, 1492-1797*. London and New York, NY: Routledge.

Hulme, Peter (1995). «Elegy for a Dying Race: The Island Caribs and their Visitors» in Neil L. Whitehead (ed.) *Wolves from the Sea*. Leiden: KITLV Press, pp. 113-138.

48

Hulme, Peter (1999). «The Rhetoric of Description: The Amerindians of the Caribbean within Modern European Discourse». *Caribbean Studies*, 23 (3-4), 35-49.

Hulme, Peter (2000). *Remnants of Conquest: The Island Caribs and Their Visitors, 1877-1998*. Oxford: Oxford University Press.

Hulme, Peter (2001). «Ethnographic Orgins: St. Vincent and Tasmania» presented at the Australian Association for Caribbean Studies conference, Canberra.

Hulme, Peter (2005). «French Accounts of the Vincentian Caribs» in Joseph O. Palacio (ed.) *The Garifuna, a Nation Across Borders: Essays in Social Anthropology*. Belize: Cubola Books, pp. 21-42.

Hulme, Peter and Neil Whitehead (eds.) (1992). *Wild Majesty*. New York: Oxford University Press.

Humphreys, Francis (1992). «The Afro-Belizean Cultural Heritage: Its Role in Combating Recolonization». *Belizean Studies*, 20 (3), 11-15.

Im Thurn, Everard F. (1883). *Among the Indians of Guiana*. London: Kegan Paul, Trench and Co.

Im Thurn, Everard F. (1967). *Among the Indians of Guiana*. New York: Dover Publications.

Instituto de Lingüística y Educación, (2004). *Glosario Bilingüe de Términos Jurídicos Español -- Garífuna = Wadimalu Disi Widü lidan Widü Hati Irumu Bian Milu Gadürü*. Guatemala: Universidad Rafael Landívar, Instituto de Defensa Pública Penal, Proyecto GUA/01/028 et al.

Izard, Gabriel (2003). «Del Colonialisme a la Defensa de la Diversitat. Cultura Garífuna i Globalització». *L'Avenç*, 286, 50-55.

Izard, Gabriel (2003). «La Construcción Política de la Identidad Garífuna en el Belice Contemporáneo». *Revista de las Américas. Historia y Presente*, 1.

Izard, Gabriel (2004). «Herencia y Etnicidad entre los Garífuna de Belice». *Revista Mexicana del Caribe*, 9 (17), 95-127.

Izard, Gabriel (2004). «Herencia, Movilizacion Social e Identidad entre los Garifunas de Belice» presented during the V Central American Anthropology Congress (Managua, Februrary 23-27, 2004), <http://www.yorku.ca/hdrnet/images/uploaded/Izard_Gabriel.pdf> viewed 6 April 2011.

Izard, Gabriel (2005). «Patrimonal Activation and Construction of Garifuna Identity in Contemporary Belize» in Joseph O. Palacio (ed.) *The Garifuna, a Nation Across Borders: Essays in Social Anthropology.* Belize: Cubola Press, pp. 176-195.

Johnson, Melissa (2003). «The Making of Race and Place in Nineteenth-Century British Honduras». *Environmental History*, 8 (4), 598-617.

Jones, Rhett S. (2001). «Black/Indian Relations: An Overview of the Scholarship». *Transforming Anthropology*, 10 (1), 2-16.

Kelly, Jerry (1996). «A Garifuna Path to Reconciliation Through Irish-American Eyes». Belize: unpublished.

Kerns, Virginia (1976). «Black Carib (Garifuna) Paternity Rituals. «*Actes du XLIIe Congres International des Americanistes*, 6, 513-524.

Kerns, Virginia (1977). *Daughters Bring in: Ceremonial and Social Organization of the Black Carib of Belize.* Ph.D. Thesis, University of Illinois, Urbana.

Kerns, Virginia (1980). «Aging and Mutual Support Relations Among the Black Carib» in Christine L. Fry (ed.) *Age in Culture and Society.* New York: Praeger, pp. 112-125.

Kerns, Virginia (1983). *Women and the Ancestors: Black Carib Kinship and Ritual.* Champaign: University of Illinois Press.

Kerns, Virginia (1984). «Past and Present Evidence of Interethnic Mating» in Michael H. Crawford (ed.) *Current Developments in Anthropological Genetics. Vol. 3: Black Caribs: A Case Study in Biocultural Adaptation,* pp. 95-114.

Kerns, Virginia (1985). «Sexuality and Social Control among the Garifuna (Belize)» in Judith K. Brown and Virginia Kerns (eds.) in *Her Prime: A New View of Middle-Aged Women.* S. Hadley, Mass: Bergin and Garvey Publishers, pp. 87-100.

Kerns, Virginia (1992). «Preventing Violence Against Women: A Central American Case» in Dorothy Ayers Counts, Judith K. Brown and Jacquelyn C. Campbell (eds.) *Sanctions and Sanctuary: Cultural Perspectives on the Beating of Wifes*. Boulder, CO: Westview Press pp. 153-167.

Kerns, Virginia (1998). «Structural Continuity in the Division of Men's and Women's Work Among the Black Carib (Garifuna)» in N.E. Whitten and A. Torres (eds.) *Blackness in Latin America and the Caribbean: Social Dynamics and Cultural Transformations: Vol. 1: Central America and Northern and Western South America*. Bloomington IN: Indiana University Press, pp. 133-148.

Khan, Aisha (1982). *Garifuna Vendedoras: Survival in the Informal Labor Sector, La Ceiba, Honduras*. M. A. Thesis, San Francisco State University.

Khan, Aisha (1987). «Migration and Life-Cycle among Garifuna (Black Carib) Street Vendors». *Women's Studies*, 13 (3), 183-98.

Lacayo Sambula, Gloria Marina (1998). *Bosquejo de la Vida del Primer Médico Garifuna de Honduras*. New York: La Sociedad Garifuna Prometra Inc.

Lafleur, Gerald (1992). *Les Caraibes des Petites Antilles*. Paris: Karthala.

Lafleur, Gerard (1996). «The Passing of a Nation: The Carib Indians of the Lesser Antilles» in Gerard Lafleur, Susan Branson, and Grace Turner (ed.) *Amerindians, Africans, Americans: Three Papers in Caribbean History*. Kingston, Jamaica: Canoe Press, pp. 3-20.

Lambey, Pablo (1992). «Traditions and Development». *Cultural Survival Quarterly*, (Fall), 41,42.

Layng, Anthony (1976). *The Carib Population of Dominica*. Ph.D. Thesis, Case Western Reserve University.

Layng, Anthony (1979). «Ethnic Identity on a West Indian Reservation». *Revista/Review Interamericana*, 9 (4), 577-584.

Le Breton, Adrien and Robert Divonne (1998). *Historic Account of St. Vincent, the Indian Youroumayn, the Island of the Karaybes*.

Mayreau Island: Mayreau Enviromental Development Organization.

Leiva Rivera, Jose Francisco (1995). *Problematica de una Comunidad Garifuna en la Costa Atlantica de Honduras.* Tesis, Escuela de Agricultura de la Región Tropical Húmeda, Guácimo (Costa Rica).

Lemmel, David Anthony (2002). *Racial Socialization and Black Identity Formation in the Initial Postsecondary School Pathways Choices in Three African-Descended Groups.* Ph.D. Thesis, University of California, Los Angeles.

López Garcia, Victor Virgilio (1993). *Lamumehan Garifuna: Clamor Garifuna.* Tornabe, Tela, Attlantida, Honduras: V.V. Lopez Garcia.

López García, Víctor Virgilo (2004). *Tradiciones Garífunas.* San Pedro Sula: Impresos Rapidos Ariel.

López Garcia, Victor Virgilio (2006). *Tornabé ante el Proyecto Turístico.* Honduras.

López Garcia, Víctor Virgilio (2007). *El Papel de la Mujer en la Cultura Garífuna.* San Pedro Sula: Impresos Rápidos Ariel.

Loveland, Christina A. and Franklin O. Loveland (1982). *Introduction in Sex Roles and Social Change in Native Lower Central American Society.* Urbana: University of Illinois Press.

Macklin, Catherine L (1986). *Crucibles of Identity: Ritual and Symbolic Dimensions of Garifuna Ethnicity.* Ph.D. Thesis, University of California, Berkeley.

Maraesa, Aminata (2009). *"I no 'fraid for that": Pregnancy, Risk, and Development in Southern Belize.* Ph.D. Thesis, New York University.

Marín, Julio César (1978). «En Busqueda de las Raices Culturales del Pueblo Garifuna». *Anuario de Estudios Centroamericanos,* 4, 569-571.

Martínez, Nancy (2006). «Ladino Blanco, Garifuna Negro. Algunos Aspectos del Racismo y la Identidad en Livingston, Guatemala» in Jose Alejos (ed.) *Dialogando alteridades. Identidades y Poder en Guatemala.* Mexico: Universidad Autónoma de México, pp.125-168.

Martínez, Nancy (2008). *La Identidad Étnica y la Identidad Nacional en la Construcción de Ciudadanía entre los Garífunas de Guatemala.* Tesis de Maestría en Antropología social, CIESAS, México, 173 p.

Massajoli, Pierleone (1971). «Popoli e Civilta dell'America Centrale: I Caribi Neri». *Universo*, 51 (4-6), 1121-1162.

Matthei, Linda and David Smith (1996). «Women, Households, and Transnational Migration Networks: The Garifuna and Global Economic Restructuring» in R. Korzeniewicz and Smith, W. (ed.) *Latin America in the World Economy.* Westport CO: Greenwood Press, pp. 133-151.

Matthei, Linda (1996). «Gender and Migration: A Networks Approach». *Social Justice*, 23 (3), 38-53.

Matthei, Linda and David Smith (1998). «Belizean Boyz 'n the Hood? Garifuna Labor Migration and Transnational Identity». *Comparative Urban and Community Research*, 6, 270-290.

Matthei, Linda M. and David A. Smith (2008). «Flexible Ethnic Identity, Adaptation, Survival, Resistance: The Garifuna in the World-system». *Social Identities*, 14 (2), 215-232.

McCauley, Ellen (1981). *No me Hables de Muerte, Sino de Parranda.* Tegucigalpa: ASEPADE (Asociación para el Desarrollo).

McClaurin, Irma (1996). *Women of Belize: Gender and Change in Central America.* New Brunswick, N.J.: Rutgers University Press.

McCommon, Carolyn (1982). *Mating as a Reproductive Strategy: A Black Carib Example.* Ph.D. Thesis, Pennsylvania State University.

McCommon, Carolyn (1989). «Refugees in Belize: A Cauldron of Ethnic Tensions» in Nancie L. Gonzalez and Carolyn S. McCommon (eds.) *Conflict, Migration, and the Expression of Ethnicity.* Boulder CO: Westview Press, pp. 91-102.

Medina, Laurie Kroshus (1992). *Power and Development: The Political Economy of Identities in Belize.* Ph.D. Thesis, University of California, Los Angeles.

Medina, Laurie Kroshus (1997). «Development Policies and Identity Politics: Class and Collectivity in Belize». *American Ethnologist*, 24 (1), 148-169.

Medina, Laurie Kroshus (2004). *Negotiating Economic Development: Identity Formation and Collective Action in Belize.* Tucson: University of Arizona Press.

Mendel, Deborah (2004). *Cultural Change in the Transnational Garifuna Community: A Case Study from Hopkins Village, Belize.* M.A. Thesis, Brown University.

Mertz, Ronald (1976). *The Effect of Father Absence on the Development of Psychological Differentiation among Male Black Carib Students in Belize.* Ph.D. Thesis, University of Arizona.

Mertz, Ronald (1977). «Psychological Differentiation among Garifuna Male Student». *Belizean Studies*, 5 (4), 17-22.

Miller, David Lawrence, 1979, David Lawernce (1979). *The European Impact on St. Vincent, 1600-1763: Suppression and Displacement of Native Population and Landscape.* M.A. Thesis University of Wisconsin, Milwaukee.

Miller, Linda Ruth (1993). *«Bridges: Garifuna Migration to Los Angeles.* Ph.D. Thesis, University of California, Irvine.

Moberg, Mark (1988). *Between Agency and Dependence: Belizean Households in a Changing World System.* Ph.D. Thesis, University of California, Los Angeles.

Moberg, Mark (1990). «Class Resistance and Class Hegemony: From Conflict to Co-operation in the Citrus Industry of Belize». *Ethnology*, 29 (3 and 4), 189-207.

Moberg, Mark (1991). «Marketing Policy and the Loss of Food Self-Sufficiency in Rural Belize». *Human Organzation*, 50 (1), 16-25.

Moberg, Mark (1992). «Structural Adjustment and Rural Development: Inferences from a Belizean Village». *The Journal of Developing Areas*, 27 (1), 1-20.

Moberg, Mark (1996). «Myths That Divide: Immigrant Labor and Class Segmentation in the Belizean Banana Industry». *American Ethnologist*, 23 (2), 311-330.

Moberg, Mark (2005). «Continuity Under Colonial Rule: The Alcalde System and the Garifuna of Belize, 1858-1969» in Joseph O. Palacio (ed.) *The Garífuna, a Nation Across Borders: Essays in Social Anthropology.* Belize: Cubola Books, pp. 85-104.

Mohr, Mauren (2001). *Lebensformen Zwischen Hier und Dort – Transnationale Migration und Wandeleiner Garífuna Gemeinde in Guatemala und New York.* Ph.D. Thesis, Universität Freiburg.

Mohr, Mauren (2003). «Migración y Cambio Socio-cultural de los Garinagu en Livingston, Izabal, Guatemala». *Tradiciones de Guatemala,* 59, 138-154.

Mohr de Collado, Mauren (2005). *Lebensformen Zwischen «Hier» und «Dort».* Bonn: Bonner Amerikanistische Studien.

Mohr de Collado, Mauren (2007). «Los Garinagu en Centroamérica y otros Lugares: Identidades de una Población Afro-Caribe entre la Tradición y la Modernidad». *Indiana,* 24, 67-86.

Mollett, Sharlene (2006). «Race and Natural Resource Conflicts in Honduras: The Miskito and Garifuna Struggle for Lasa Pulan». *Latin American Research Review,* 41 (1), 76-103.

Monsalve, M.V. and E. Hagelberg (1997). «Mitochondrial DNA Polymorphisms in Carib People of Belize». *Proceedings: Biological Sciences,* 264 (1385), 1217-1224.

Moore, Richard B. (1973). «Carib 'Cannibalism': A Study in Anthropological Stereotyping». *Caribbean Studies,* 13, 117-135.

Morales, F. and Nelly Arvelo Jimenez (1981). «Hacia un Modelo de Estructura Social Caribe». *America Indigena,* 41 (4), 603-625.

Moreau, Jean-Pierre (1991). «Les Caraibes Insulaires et la Mer aux XVIIe Siecles d'apres les Sources Ethnohistoriques». *Journal de Societe des Americanistes,* 77, 63-75.

Munroe, Robert L. (1964). *Couvade Practices of the Black Carib: A Psychological Study.* Ph.D. Thesis, Harvard University.

Munroe, Robert L. (1980). «Male Transvestism and the Couvade: A Psycho-Cultural Analysis». *Ethos,* 8 (1), 49-59.

Munroe, Robert L. (2001). «Father Absence, Social Structure, and Attention Allocation in Children: A Four-Culture Comparison». *Ethos*, 29 (3), 315-328.

Munroe, Robert L. (2004). «Social Structure and Sex-Role Choices Among Children in Four Cultures». *Cross-Cultural Research: The Journal of Comparative Social Science*, 38 (4), 387-406.

Munroe, Robert L. and Ruth H. Munroe (1969). «A Cross-Cultural Study of Sex Gender and Social Structure». *Ethnology*, 8 (2), 206-211.

Munroe, Robert L. and Ruth H. Munroe (1971). «Male Pregnancy Symptoms and Cross-sex Identity in Three Societies». *Journal of Social Psychology*, 84, 11-25.

Munroe, Robert L. and Ruth H. Munroe (1973). «Psychological Interpretation of Male Initiation Rites: The Case of Male Pregnancy Symptoms». *Ethos*, 1 (4), 490-498.

Munroe, Robert L., Ruth H. Munroe, and John Whiting, (1973). «The Couvade: A Psychological Analysis». *Ethos*, 1 (1), 30-74.

Murschhauser, Marc (2009). Garínagu: Die Schwarzen Kariben von Honduras von Kultureller Dynamik und Nostalgie. <http://www.uni-hamburg.de/ethnologie/es11_1_artikel.pdf> viewed 31 June 2011.

Nas, Peter J. M. (2002). «CA Forum on Anthropology in Public: Masterpieces of Oral and Intangible Culture: Reflections on the UNESCO World Heritage List». *Current Anthropology*, 43 (1), 139-148.

Neckebrouck, Valeer (2002). *Zwarte Indianen en hun Symbolen: het Magische-Religieuze Systeem van de Garifuna van de Baai van Tela, Honduras*. Dudley, Mass: Peeters.

Nedwed, Alina (2009). *Spiritualitat und Identitat in Garifuna-Gemeinden in Belize und Guatemala*. Magistra der Philosophie Thesis, Universität Wien.

Noe, Susan Y. (2001). «Land Rights of the Garifuna of Belize: A Preliminary Analysis under Domestic and International Law» prepared for the National Garifuna Council.

Norales, F. O. (2003). «The Garifuna Culture: A Proclaimed Masterpiece in Central America». *Journal of Intergroup Relations*, 30 (2), 35-46.

Obando Sancho, V. and et al. (1999). *Orinoco: Revitalización Cultural de Pueblo Garífuna de la Costa Caribe Nicaragüense*. Managua: URACCAN Bluefields.

Ochoa Moreno, Donaldo (2003). *Estudio Diagnóstico sobre la Situación de la Tenencia de la Tierra de los Pueblos Indígenas y Garífuna*. Tegucigalpa: Comisionado Nacional de los Derechos Humanos.

Olawaiye, James Adeyinka (1980). *Yoruba Religious and Social Traditions in Ekite, Nigeria and Three Caribbean Countries: Trinidad-Tobago, Guyana and Belize*. Ph.D. Thesis, University of Missouri in Kansas City.

Owens, Nancy H. (1975). «Land, Politics and Ethnicity in a Carib Indian Community». *Ethnology*, 14 (4), 385-93.

Owens, Nancy H. (1980). «Conflict and Ethnic Boundaries: A Study of Carib-Black Relations». *Social and Economic Studies*, 29 (2-3), 264-274.

Palacio, Joseph O. (1975). «Problems in the Maintenance of the Garifuna (Black Carib) Culture in Belize» presented in the Symposium Black Adaptive Strategies for Survival 1975 American Anthropological Association Meetings, San Francisco.

Palacio, Joseph O. (1982). *Food and Social Relations in a Garifuna Village*. Ph.D. Thesis, University of California, Berkeley.

Palacio, Joseph O. (1983). «Food and Body in Garifuna Belief Systems». *Cajanus*, 16 (3), 149-160.

Palacio, Joseph O. (1984). «Food and Social Relations in a Belizean Garifuna Village». *Belizean Studies*, 12 (3), 1-7.

Palacio, Joseph O. (1984). «Food Exchange Systems». *Belizean Studies*, 12 (3), 12-32.

Palacio, Joseph O. (1987). «Age as Source of Differentiation within a Garifuna Village in Southern Belize». *America Indigena*, 47 (1), 97-119.

Palacio, Joseph O. (1988). «Social and Cultural Differences in Belize: The Genesis of Ethnicity and Nation-State in the Caribbean Coast of Central America». *Estudios Sociales Centroamericanos*, 48, 125-141.

Palacio, Joseph O. (1989). «Caribbean Indigenous Peoples Jouirney toward Self-Discovery». *Cultural Survival Quarterly*, 13 (8), 49-51.

Palacio, Joseph O. (1989). «The Sojourn toward Self-Discovery among Caribbean Indigenous Peoples». *Saskatchewan Indian Federared College Journal*, 5 (1), 41-64.

Palacio, Joseph O. (1991). «Kin Ties, Food, Remittances in a Garifuna Village in Southern Belize» in Anne Sharman et al (eds.) *Diet and Domestic Life in Society*. Philadelphia: Temple University Press, pp. 119-146.

Palacio, Joseph O. (1992). «Garifuna Immigrants in Los Angeles: Attempts at Self-Improvement». *Belizean Studies*, 20 (3), 17-26.

Palacio, Joseph O. (1992). «The Sojourn toward Self-Discovery among Caribbean Indigenous Peoples». *Caribbean Quarterly*, 38 (3-4), 55-72.

Palacio, Joseph O. (1992). «What Rural People are Saying about Rural Community Development» *SPEAReports 8 Independence Ten Years After*. Belize: SPEAR, pp. 127-143.

Palacio, Joseph O. (1993). «Social and Cultural Implications of Recent Demographic Changes in Belize». *Belizean Studies*, 21 (3), 3-12.

Palacio, Joseph O. (1993). «Survival, Recognition, Reparation». *The Second Gathering. Proceedings of Symposia, Aug. 31 - Sep. 02, 1993,* , 3-7.

Palacio, Joseph O. (1996). «Is There a Future for Africanness in Belize?». *UCB Journal of Belizean Affairs*, 1 (1), 34-47.

Palacio, Joseph O. (1998). «Cultural Retrieval among the Garifuna in Belize: An Exercise in Continuing Education». *Caribbean Quarterly*, 44 (3 and 4), 50-62.

Palacio, Joseph O. (1998). «Reconstructing Garifuna Oral History – techniques and methods in the story of a Caribbean people». *Journal of Eastern Caribbean Studies,* 24 (1), 1-24.

Palacio, Joseph O. (2000). «A Reconsideration of the Native American and African Roots of Garifuna Identity» presented at Professional Agricultural Workers Conference, 58th Session, Tuskegee University, 3-5 December.

Palacio, Joseph O. (2000). «From One Brink to Another: Aboriginal Peoples in CARICOM at the Close of the 20th Century». *CARICOM Perspective,* 2 (69), 87-91.

Palacio, Joseph O. (2001). «Coastal Traditional Knowledge and Cultural Values: Their Significance to The Garifuna and the Rest of the Region» presented UWI School of Continuing Studies» Beyond Walls: Multi-Disciplinry Perspectives» .

Palacio, Joseph O. (2002). «Past and Current Methods of Community-Based Coastal Resource Management in Southern Belize» in IDRC-CBCRM (ed.) *Balancing People and Resources – Interdisciplinary Research and Coastal Areas Management in the Wider Caribbean.* Heredia, Costa Rica: Editorial Fundacion UNA, pp. 257-277.

Palacio, Joseph O. (2003). «Why are Some Garifuna Students Underachieving in Primary and Secondary Schools?». *Belizean Studies,* 25 (2).

Palacio, Joseph O. (2004). «Caribbean Organization of Indigenous Peoples (COIP): Contribution to the Indigenous Peoples› Movement in the Caribbena and Americas» Manuscript 1090, National Anthropological Archives, Smithsonian Institution.

Palacio, Joseph O. (2005). «Building Sustainable Livielihoods for the Food Insecure and Nutritionally Vulnerable in Belize». *Belizean Studies,* 27 (1), 26-76.

Palacio, Joseph O. (2005). «Reconstructing Garifuna Oral History: Techniques and Methods in the History of a Caribbean People» in Joseph O. Palacio (ed.) *The Garifuna, a Nation Across Borders: Essays in Social Anthropology.* Belize: Cubola Books, pp. 43-63.

Joseph O. Palacio (ed.) (2005). *The Garifuna, a Nation Across Borders: Essays in Social Anthropology.* Belize: Cubola Books.

Palacio, Joseph O. (2006). "Looking at Ourselves in the Mirror: The Caribbean Organization of Indigenous Peoples» in Maximilian C. Forte (ed.) *Indigenous Resurgence in the Contemporary Caribbean.* New York: Peter Lang, pp. 215-223.

Palacio, Joseph O. (2006). «Territoriality, Technical Revitalization, and Symbolism in Garifuna and Kuna Indigenous Communities of Belize, Guatemala, and Panama» in Yvan Breton, David Brown, Brian Davy, Milton Haughton and Luis Ovares (ed.) *Coastal Resource Management in the Wider Caribbean: Resilience, Adaptation, and Community Diversity.* Kingston, Jamaica: Ian Randle Publishers, pp. 78-104.

Palacio, Joseph O. (2007). «How Did the Garifuna become an Indigenous People? Reconstructing the Cultural Persona of an African-Native American People in Central America». Revista Pueblos y Fronteras, 4 <http://redalyc.uaemex.mx/ redalyc/src/inicio/ArtPdfRed.jsp?iCve=90600412> viewed 11 April 2011.

Palacio, Joseph O., Judy Lumb and Carlson Tuttle (2009). «Transmission of Rights to House Lots in Barranco, a Garifuna Village in Southern Belize 1895 to 2000» in Elisabeth Cunin and Odile Hoffmann (coord.) *Etnicidad y Nacion: Debate Alrededor do Belice, Belize: Ethnicity and Nation.* Mexico City: AFRODESC, Working Paper No. 5, pp. 87-115.

Palacio, Joseph O., Judith Rae Lumb and Carlson Tuttle (2010). «El Poder de la Demarcación: El Primer Deslindamiento en Barranco, Belice» in Odile Hoffmann (ed.) *Politica e Identidad, Afrodescendientes en Mexico y America Central.* Mexico City: CEMCA, CNCA, IRD, INAH, UNAM, pp. 189-231.

Palacio, Joseph O., Judith Rae Lumb and Carlson Tuttle (2011). *Garifuna Continuity in Land: Barranco Settlement and Land Use 1862 to 2000.* Caye Caulker, Belize: Producciones de la Hamaca.

Palacio, Myrtle (1995). *Redefining Ethnicity. The Experiences of the Garifuna and Creole in Post-Independent Belize.* M.S. Thesis, University of New Orleans.

Palacio, Myrtle (2000). «Food Security and the Poverty Paradox at the Local Level: The Case of North/South Belize». Presented at International Food and Nutrition Conference, Tuskegee University. Tuskegee, Alabama, October 8-10.

Palacio, Myrtle (2001). «Dangriga, BZ or USA?: Out-migration Experiences of a Garifuna Community in Post-independent Belize». Presented at the University of the West Indies Belize Country Conference, November 21-24. <uwichill.edu.bb/bnccde/belize/conference/Papers/palaciom.html> viewed 11 April 2011

Palacio-Cayetano, Joycelin (1998). *Hagana san Linebafan Chatoyer Larigi Bian San Irumu?* Belize City: unpublished.

Parker, John D. (2008). «A Garifuna Case Study from Roatan Island, Honduras» in Tomas Alberto Avila and Jose Francisco Avila (ed.) *Garifuna World.* Providence: Milenio Associates, LLC, pp. 117-140.

Pastora, Carla (1999). *Expulsion, Displacement, Colonization and Survival: The Untold History of the Garifunas and Their Gubidas.* M.A. Thesis, East Carolina State University.

Payne Iglesias, Elizet (2001). «Identidad y Nación: el Caso de la Costa Norte e Islas de la Bahía en Honduras, 1876–1930». *Mesoamerica,* 22 (42), 75-103.

Payne Iglesias, Elizet (2004). «Poblacion, Diversidad Étnic y Sociedad en Truxillo (1821)» VII Congreso Centroamericano De Historia Universidad Nacional Autónoma de HondurasTegucigalpa, <http://www.centroamerica.fcs.ucr.ac.cr/Contenidos/hca/cong/mesas/cong7/.../1_12.doc> viewed 14 January 2011.

Payne Iglesias, Elizet (2005). *El Puerto de Truxillo. Espacio, Economia y Sociedad, 1780-1870.* Tesis Doctoral, Universidad de Costa Rica.

Payne Iglesias, Elizet (2007). *El Puerto de Truxillo. Un Viaje Hacia su Melancólico Abandono.* Tegucigalpa: Editorial Guaymuras.

Perdomo, Marcella (2004). *Etude Comparative du Rite Dügu des Garifunas.* (DEA) Master II, Université Paris III – IHEAL.

Perdomo, Marcella (2005). *La Punta, Danse Rituelle/Danse Spectacle: Tourisme et Identité Dans la Communauté Garifuna de Roatan.* Master I, Université Paris III – IHEAL.

Perdomo, Marcella (2008). *Le Culte des Ancêtres Gubida. La Tradition Rituelle des Garifunas.* Master Ecole des Hautes Etudes en Sciences Sociales – EHESS.

Perry, Marc D. (1998). «New York City Garifuna and Multiple Imagings of Diasporic Blackness» presented at American Anthropological Association Annual Meeting, Washington D.C.

Perry, Marc D. (1998). «Racial and Gendered Performance among Garifuna Youth in New York City» invited lecture in Introduction to Cultural Anthropology taught by Dr. Jane Henrici, University of Texas.

Perry, Marc D. (1999). *Garifuna Youth in New York City: Race, Ethnicity, and the Performance of Diasporic Identities.* M.A. Thesis, University of Texas at Austin.

Perry, Pamela (1990). *«Subordinate to No One» Practice, Consciousness and Garifuna Response to the Sandinista Revolution.* M.A. Thesis, University of Texas at Austin.

Perry, Pamela (1991). «Collective Identity and the Politics of Etnicity: The Case Study of a Pro-Sadinista Community on the Atlantic Coast of Nicaragua» submitted to the Sociology Department and the Graduate Division of University of California at Berkeley.

Porter, Robert W. (1983). «El Estilo Migratorio de Vida en la Biografía Garífuna». *Yaxkin,* 6 (1-2), 56-65.

Portillo Villeda, Suyapa G. (2010). «The Coup That Awoke a People's Resistance». *NACLA Report on the Americas,* 43 (2), 26-27.

Ramsdell, L. (2008). «The Mythical Return to the Mother (land): Cinematic Representations of the Garifuna and Cuban Diasporas». *Hispanic Journal,* 29 (2), 115-126.

Rauch, Molly Elissa (1992). «Making Ereba: Networks of Exchange among the Bakers of Barranco» presented for Independent Study Project.

Rey, Nicolas (2005). «Caraïbes Noirs et "Negros Franceses" (Antilles/Amérique Centrale): Le Périple de Noirs "Révolutionnaires"» Nouveau Monde Mondes Nouveaux, <http://nuevomundo.revues.org/315> viewed 11 April 2011.

Rey, Nicolas (2005). «Les Garifunas: Entre Mémoire de la Résistance aux Antilles et Transmission des Terres en Amérique Centrale». Cahiers d'Etudes Africaines, 177, 152-155.

Rey, Nicolas (2010). «La Movilización de los Garífunas para Preservar sus Tierras "Ancestrales» en Guatemala». Revista Pueblos y Fronteras digital 5, (8), 30-59. <http://www.pueblosyfronteras.unam.mx/a09n8/pdfs/n8_art02.pdf> viewed 6 January 2012.

Rey, Nicolas (2011). «Amérique Centrale: La Lutte des Garifunas pour l'Identité et la Terre, Face au Tourisme» in Nicoles Rey et al., Tourisme Durable et Patrimoines. Une dialectique développementale? (Europe-Caraïbe-Amériques-Afrique-Asie). Paris: Karthala, pp. 219-242.

Rivas, Ramon D. (1993). Pueblos Indigenas y Garifuna de Honduras. Tegucigalpa: Editorial Guaymuras.

Riviére, P.G. (1974). «The Couvade: A Problem Reborn». Man, 9, 423-435.

Roberts, Derek F. (1984). «Anthropogenetics in a Hybriud Population: The Black Carib Studies» in Michael H. Crawford (ed.) Current Developments in Anthropological Genetics. Vol. 3: Black Caribs: A Case Study in Biocultural Adaptation. New York: Plenum Press, pp. 381-387.

Robiou-Lamarche, Sebastian (1990). «Island Carib Mythology and Astronomy». Journal of Latin American Indian Literatures, 6 (1), 36-54.

Roessingh, Carel Henning (1998). De Belizaanse Garifuna: de Contouren van een Etnische Gemeenschap in Middel-Amerika = The Belizean Garifuna: the Contours of an Ethnic Community in Central America. Ph.D. Thesis, Uneversiteit Utrecht.

Roessingh, Carel (2001). The Belizean Garifuna. Amsterdam: Rozenberg.

Roessingh, Carel and Karin Bras (2003). «Garifuna Settlement Day: Tourism Attraction, National Celebration Day, or Manifestation of Ethnic Identity?». *Tourism Culture and Communication*, 4 (3), 163-172.

Rojas Silva, Bienvenido (2003). *El Silencio de los Garífunas*. La Habana: Pablo de la Torriente.

Roth, Walter E. (1915). "An Inquiry into the Animism and Folk-lore of the Guiana Indians». *Thirtieth Annual Report of the Bureau of American Ethnology, 1908-1909*, pp. 103-386.

Rouse, Irving (1963). «The Caribs» in Julian H. Steward (ed.) *Handbook of South American Indians*, Vol. 4, *the Circum-Caribbean Tribes*, pp. 547-565.

Rouse, Irving (1991). *The Taino: Rise and Fall of the People who Greeted Columbus*. New Haven: Yale University Press.

Ruiz Alvarez, Santiago Jaime (2008). *Preservation Strategies of the Garifuna Language in the Context of Global Economy in the Village of Corozal in Honduras*. Ph.D. Thesis, University of Florida.

Rust, Susie Post (2001). «The Garifuna: Weaving a Future from a Tangled Past». *National Geographic Magazine*, 202 (10), 102-113.

Sabin, Miriam, George Luber, Keith Sabin, Mayte Paredes, and Edgar Monterroso (2008). «Rapid Ethnographic Assessment of HIV/AIDS among Garifuna Communities in Honduras: Informing HIV Surveillance among Garfiuna Women». *Journal of Human Behavior in the Social Environment*, 17 (3-4), 237-257.

Sabio, Fernando andf Celia Karina Ordóñez (2006). *Hererun Wagüchagu: Dimurei-agei Garifuna*. La Ceiba: Asociación Misionera Garifuna de Honduras.

Salamanca, D. (1993). «Los Idiomas Indigenas y de la Poblacion Negra de Nicaragua». *América Indígena*, 53 (1-2), 23-40.

Salas, Antonio and Martin Richards et al (2005). «Shipwrecks and Founder Effects: Divergent Demographic Histories Reflected in Caribbean mtDNA». *American Journal of Physical Anthropology*, 128 (4), 855-860.

Sanford, Margaret (1971). *Disruption of the Mother-child Relationship in Conjunction with Matrifocality: A Study of Child-keeping among the Carib and Creole of British Honduras.* Ph.D. Thesis, Catholic University.

Sanford, Margaret (1974). «Child-lending in a British West Indian Society». *Ethnology*, 13 (4), 393-400.

Sanford, Margaret (1974). «Revitalization Movements as Indicators of Completed Acculturation». *Comparative Studies in Society and History*, 16, 504-518.

Sanford, Margaret (1975). «To Be Treated as a Child of the Home: Black Carib Child Lending in a British West Indian Society» in Thomas R. Williams (ed.) *Socialization and Communication in Primary Groups.* The Hague: Mouton, pp. 159-181.

Sanford, Margaret (1976). «Child Lending in Belize». *Belizean Studies*, 4 (2), 26-36.

Sanford, Margaret (1976). «Disease and Folk-curing among the Garifuna of Belize». *Actes du XLIIe Congres International des Americanistes*, 6, 553-560.

Sapper, Karl (1893). *Beiträge zur Ethnographie der Republik Guatemala.* Gotha: H. Haack.

Sapper, Karl (1897). «Mittelamericanische Caraiben». *Internationales Archiv fur Ethnographie*, 10, 53-68.

Sapper, Karl (1905). *Den Vulcangebieten Mittelamerikas und Westindiens.* Stuttgart: Verlag der E. Schweizerbartschen Verlagsbuchhandlung.

Seitz, Karl Steven (2005). *Migration, Demographic Change, and the Enigma of Identity in Belize.* M.A. Thesis, Arizona State University.

Serna Moreno, J. Jesus (2006). «Garífuna, Garínagu, Caribe». *Archipiélago. Revista Cultural de Nuestra América*, 8 (37), 65.

Servio-Mariano, Boyd Malcolm (2010). *Garifunaduau: Cultural Continuity, Change and Resistance in the Garifuna Diaspora.* Ph.D. Thesis, State University of New York at Albany.

Smith, Frederick H. (2006). «European Impressions of the Island Carib's Use of Alcohol in the Early Colonial Period». *Ethnohistory*, 53 (3), 543-566.

Smith, Malinda Sharon (1993). *Power, Ideology and the Construction of the Contra/Revolution (Nicaragua)*. Ph.D. Thesis, University of Alberta.

Sociedad Bíblica de Nueva York Internacional, (1988). *Lererun Bungiu To Lanina Iseri Daradu*. East Brunswick, N.J.

Solares, Jorge (1993). *Estado y Nación: las Demandas de los Grupos Étnicos en Guatemala*. Guatemala: FLACSO-Guatemala p. 468.

Soley, R.M. (1989). «Religion and Traditional Medicine among the Garifuna of Nicaragua». *Estudios Sociales Centroamericanos*, 51 (Sept-Dec), 117-123.

Soliens, Nancie L. (1959). *The Consanguineal Household among the Black Carib of Central America*. Ph.D. Thesis, University of Michigan.

Soliens, Nancie L. (1959). «West Indian Characteristics of the Black Caribs». *Southwest Journal of Anthropology*, 15 (3), 300-307.

Soliens, Nancie L. (1960). «Changes in Black Carib Kinship Terminology». *Southwestern Journal of Anthropology*, 16 (2), 144-159.

Staiano, Kathryn Vance (1981). «Alternative Therapeutic Systems in Belize: A Semiotic Framework». *Social Science and Medicine*, 15, 317-332.

Staiano, Kathryn Vance (1986). *Interpreting Signs of Illness: A Case Study in Medical Semiotics*. Berlin: Mouton de Gruyter.

Steward, Julian H. and Louis C. Faron (1959). *Native Peoples of South America*. New York: McGraw-Hill Book Company.

Stoll, Otto (1884). *Zur Ethnographie der Republik Guatemala*. Zürich: Orell Füssli.

Stone, Michael Cutler (1990). «The Afro-Caribbean Presence in Central America». *Belizean Studies*, 18 (2-3), 6-42.

Straughan, Jerome F. (2004). *Belizean Immigrants in Los Angeles.* Ph.D. Thesis, University of Southern California.

Suazo, Salvador (1996). *La Sociedad Garífuna: Un Vistazo sobre el Estilo de Vida Garífuna = Adámuri Garífuna: Murusun Aríhini luagu Laníchigu Garífuna.* Tegucigalpa: CEDEC-Bilance.

Suazo, Salvador (1999). *Uraga: la Tradición Oral del Pueblo Garífuna = Uraga: Aban Echuni Ichíguti Resun hadan Garinagu.* Tegucigalpa: CEDEC: Bilance/CORDAID.

Suazo, Salvador (2000). *Haun Damusianu: el Almanaque Garífuna 2000.* Tegucigalpa: CEDEC, Centro de Desarrollo Comunitario.

Taylor, Douglas MacRae (1938). «The Caribs of Dominica». *Bureau of American Ethnology Bulletin, Anthropological Papers, No. 3,* 119, 103-159.

Taylor, Douglas MacRae (1941). «Columbus Saw Them First». *Natural History,* 48, 41-50.

Taylor, Douglas MacRae (1945). «Carib Folk Beliefs and Customs from Dominica, British West Indies». *Southwestern Journal of Anthropology,* 1 (4), 507-30.

Taylor, Douglas MacRae (1946). «Kinship and Social Structure of the Island Carib». *Southwestern Journal of Anthropology,* 2 (2), 180-212.

Taylor, Douglas MacRae (1946). «Notes on the Star Lore of the Caribbees». *American Anthropologist,* 48 (2), 215-222.

Taylor, Douglas MacRae (1948). «Conversation and Letter from the Black Carib of British Honduras». *International Journal of American Language and Linguistics,* 14 (2), 99-107.

Taylor, Douglas MacRae (1949). «The Interpretation of Some Documentary Evidence on Carib Culture». *Southwestern Journal of Anthropology,* 5 (4), 379-392.

Taylor, Douglas MacRae (1950). «The Meaning of Dietary and Occupational Restrictions among the Island Carib». *American Anthropologist,* 52 (3), 343-349.

Taylor, Douglas MacRae (1951). *The Black Caribs of British Honduras*. New York: Viking Fund Publications in Anthropology.

Taylor, Douglas MacRae (1952). «Tales and Legends of the Dominica Caribs». *Journal of American Folklore*, 65 (257), 267-279.

Taylor, Douglas MacRae (1953). «A Note on Marriage and Kinship Among the Island Carib». *Man*, 53 (August), 117-119.

Taylor, Douglas MacRae (1965). «A Biased View: A Rebuttal to Solien». *American Anthropologist*, 67 (6, part 1), 1524-1526.

Thorne, Eva T. (2005). «Land Rights and Garifuna Identity». *NACLA Report on the Americas*, 38 (2), 21-25.

Tompson, Doug (2004). «Useful Laborers and Savage Hordes: Hispanic Central American Views of Afro-Indigenous Peoples in the Nineteenth Century». *Transforming Anthropology*, 12 (1-2), 21-29.

Trautmann, Rita (2007). «Der Mann und das Meer, die Frau und das Land... Geschlechterspezifischer Umgang mit dem Landkonflikt bei den Garínagu in Iriona, Honduras» in Rossbach de Olmos, Lioba und Heike Drotbohm (ed.) *Afroamerikanische Kontroversen. Beiträge der Regionalgruppe "Afroamerika" auf der Tagungder Deutschen Gesellschaft für Völkerkunde in Halle (Saale) 2005*. Marburg: Curupira, pp. 101-118.

Valencia Chala, S. (2006). *Blacks in Central America*. Lewiston, N.Y. Queenston, Ontario: Edwin Mellen Press.

Valentine, Jerris (2002). *The Garifuna Understanding of Death*. Dangriga, Belize: National Garifuna Council.

Verin, Pierre (1964). *La Pointe Caraibe, Sainte-Lucie*. M.A. Thesis, Yale University.

Verin, Pierre (1966). «L'Ancienne Culture Caraibe a l'Epoque Coloniale». *Bulletin de la Societe d'Histoire de la Guadeloupe*, 5-6, 16-26.

Verin, Pierre (1967). «Carib Culture in Colonial Times». *International Congress for the Study of Pre-Columbian Cultures in the Lesser Antilles*, 115-120.

Vernon, Lawrence (1964). *A Brief Ethnological Description of Belizean Races*. Belmopan: National Archives.

Vilas, Carlos M. (1989). *State, Class and Ethnicity in Nicaragua*. Boulder,CO: Lynne Rienner.

Walker, Jeff and Richard Wilk (1989). «The Manufacture and Use-Wear Characteristics of Ethnographic, Replicated, and Archaeological Manioc Grater Board Teeth» in Margarita Gaxiola G. and John E. Clark (eds.) *La Obsidiana en Mesoamérica*. Tegucigalpa: Instituto Nacional de Antropologia e Historia, pp. 459-463.

Wells, Marilyn Mckillop (1982). «Dugu Visibility: The Role of a Religious Ceremony in Status Politics». *Tennessee Anthropologist*, 7 (1), 75-88.

Wells, Marilyn McKillop (1982). «The Symbolic Use of Guseue Among the Garif (Black Carib) Central America». *Anthropological Quarterly*, 55 (1), 44-55.

Weymes, H and H. Gershowitz (1984). «Genetic Structure of the Garifuna Population in Belize» in Michael H. Crawford (ed.) *Current Developments in Anthropological Genetics*. Vol. 3: *Black Caribs: A Case Study in Biocultural Adaptation*. New York: Plenum Press, pp. 365-379.

White, Leland Ross (1969). *The Development of More Open Racial and Ethnic Relations in British Honduras during the Nineteenth Century*. Ph.D. Thesis, University of Missouri, Columbia.

Whitehead, Neil Lancelot (1990). «Carib Ethnic Soldiering in Venezuela, the Guianas, and the Antilles, 1492-1820». *Ethnohistory*, 37 (4), 357-385.

Whitehead, Neil L. (1995). *Wolves from the Sea*. Leiden: KITLV Press. Whitten, Norman and Rachel Corr (2001). «Contesting the Images of Oppression: Indigenous Views of Blackness in the Americas». *NACLA Report on the Americas*, 34 (6), 24-28.

Wilcox, Sharon Elizabeth (2006). *Reconstructing Identity: Representational Strategies in the Garifuna Community of Dangriga, Belize*. M.A. Thesis, University of Texas at Austin.

Wilk, Richard and Mac Chapin (1990). *Ethnic Minorities in Belize: Mopan, Kekchi and Garifuna*. Belize City: SPEAR.

Wilk, Richard (1997). «Rituals of Difference and Identity: Connecting the Global and the Local» Presented to the Ph.D. Course 'Modern Times, Modern Rituals'. Department of Ethnography and Social Anthropology,University of Aarhus (Denmark) November 1997, <http://indiana.academia.edu/ RichardWilk/Papers/172865/Rituals_of_Difference_and_ Identity_Connecting_the_Global_and_the_Local> viewed 1 February 2011.

Wilson, Samuel (ed.) (1997). *The Indigenous People of the Caribbean.* Gainesville: University Press of Florida.

Witty, Karen (2010). *Income and Ethnicity as Predictors of Sexual Behavior in Belize, Central America: A Community Survey.* Ph.D. Thesis, Walden University.

Woods, Louis A. and Joseph M. Perry, Jeffrey W. Steagall (1997). «The Composition and Distribution of Ethnic Groups in Belize: Immigration and Emigration Patterns, 1980-1991». *Latin American Research Review,* 32 (3), 63-88.

Education / Education/ Educación

Achtem, Janice (2010). *Collectively Coming to Know: An Ethnographic Study of Teacher Learning in Toledo, Belize.* Ph.D. Thesis, University of Victoria.

Freeland, Jane (2003). «Intercultural-Bilingual Education for an Interethnic-Plurilingual Society? The Case of Nicaragua's Caribbean Coast». *Comparative Education,* 39 (2), 239-260.

Freeland, Jane (1999). «Can the Grass Roots Speak? The Literacy Campaign in English on Nicaragua's Atlantic Coast». *International Journal of Bilingual Education and Bilingualism,* 2 (3), 214-232.

Haug, Sarah Woodbury (1998). «Ethnicity and Ethnically Mixed Identity in Belize: A Study of Primary School-Age Children». *Anthropology and Education Quarterly,* 29 (1), 44-67.

Joseph, Vilma Linett (2003). *Differential Performance in English Tests among Different Language Groups: Sociolinguistic Study of Belizean Speech Communities.* Ph.D. Thesis, University of Kansas.

Kleyn, Tatyana (2010). «Cultural Mismatch in Honduran Garifuna Communities: The Role of Culture, Race, and Language in Schools». *Diaspora, Indigenous, and Minority Education,* 4 (4), 217-234.

Murphy-Graham, Erin (2008). «Opening the Black Box: Women's Empowerment and Innovative Secondary Education in Honduras». *Gender and Education,* 20 (1), 31-50.

Murphy-Graham, Erin (2010). «And when She Comes Home? Education and Women's Empowerment in Intimate Relationships». *International Journal of Educational Development,* 30 (3), 320-331.

Ethnohistory / Ethnohistoire / Etnohistoria

Anderson, Susan Heller (1969). «Three Relations of the West Indies in 1659-1660, de Cosimo Brunetti». *Transactions of the American Philosophical Society*, 59 (6), 1-49.

Arrivillaga Cortés, Alfonso (1988). «Documentos Para el Estudio de la Historia Popular de los Caribes Negros de Livingston, Guatemala». *Tradiciones de Guatemala*, 30, 131-137.

Bateman, Rebecca B, (1981). «African Frontiersmen: The Black Carib of St. Vincent Island». *Papers in Anthropology*, 22 (1), 119-130.

Bateman, Rebecca B. (1990). «Africans and Indians: A Comparative Study of the Black Carib and Black Seminole». *Ethnohistory*, 37 (1), 1-24.

Benoît, Catherine (1997). «Nueva Evidencia sobre el Origen de los Caribes Negros, con Consideraciones sobre el Significado de la Tradicion». *Cahiers d'Études Africaines*, 37 (148), 863-890.

Borde, de la (1886). «History of the Origin, Customs, Religion, Wars, and Travels of the Caribs, Savages of the Antilles in America». Timehri, 5, 224-253.

Boucher, Philip (1992). *Cannibal Encounters: Europeans and the Island Caribs, 1492-1763*. Baltimore: John Hopkins University Press.

Cheek, Charles (1986). «Black Carib Settlement Patterns in Early 18th Century Honduras: The Search for a Livelyhood». *Ethnohistory: A Researcher's Guide, Studies in Third World Societies*. Williamsburg, VA: Department of Anthropology, College of William and Mary, pp. 403-429.

Davidson, William V. (1980). «The Garifuna of Pearl Lagoon: Ethnohistory of an Afro-American Enclave in Nicaragua». *Ethnohistory*, 27 (1), 31-47.

Davidson, William V. (1983). «Ethnohistoria Hondurena: La Llegada de los Garifunas a Honduras, 1797». *Yaxkin*, VI (1-2), 88-105.

Debbasch, Yvan (1961). «Le Marronnage: Essai sur la Desertion de L'Esclave Antillais». *L'Annee Sociologique*, 1-45.

Forte, Maximilian C. (2003). «How The Amerindians of Arima Lost Their Lands: Notes from Primary and Other Historical Sources, 1802-1879». *Issues in Caribbean Amerindian Studies (Occasional Papers of the Caribbean Amerindian Centrelink)*, 5 (1), 1-38.

González, Nancie L. (1986). «Garifuna Traditions in Historical Perspective». *Belizean Studies*, 14 (2), 11-24.

González, Nancie L. (1987). «Garifuna Traditions in Historical Perspective» in Lita Hunter Krohn (ed.) *Readings in Belizean History, 2nd edition.* Belize City: St. John's College Press, pp. 122-130.

González, Nancie L. (1988). *Sojourners of the Caribbean: Ethnogenesis and Ethnohistory of the Garifuna.* Urbana: University of Illinois Press.

González, Nancie L. (1990). «From Cannibals to Mercenaries: Carib Militarism, 1600-1840». *Journal of Anthropological Research*, 46 (1), 25-39.

González, Nancie L, (2008). *Peregrinos del Caribe. Etnogénesis y Etnohistoria de los Garifunas.* Tegucigalpa: Editorial Guaymuras.

Gullick, Charles J.M.R.C. (1976). «Black Carib Orgins and Early Society». *International Congress for the Study of Pre-Columbian Cultures of the Lesser Antilles*, 5-7, 283-290.

Helbig, Karl (1965). *Areas y Paisajes del Noreste de Honduras.* Tegucigalpa. Honduras: Banco Central de Honduras.

Honychurch, Lennox (1997). *Carib to Creole: A History of Contact and Culture Exchange.* Ph.D. Thesis, University of Oxford.

Hulme, Peter (1978). «Columbus and the Cannibals: A Study of the Reports of Anthropophagy in the Journal of Christopher Columbus». *IberoAmerikanisches Archiv*, 4, 115-139.

Hulme, Peter (2000). «Travel, Ethnography, Transculturation: St. Vincent of the 1790s» presented at the conference, Contextualizing the Caribbean, U of Miami, Coral Gables.

Hunter, John M. and Renate de Kleine (1984). «Geophagy in Central America». *Geographical Review*, 74 (2), 157-169.

Layng, Anthony (1985). «The Caribs of Dominica: Prospects for Structural Assimilation of a Territorial Minority». *Ethnic Groups*, 6 (2-3), 209-221.

Mathieu, Nicolas del Castillo (1975). «Lexico Caribe en el Caribe Negro de Honduras Britanica». *Thesaurus*, 30 (3 and 4), 401-470.

Moberg, Mark (1992). «Continuity Under Colonial Rule: the Alcade System and the Garifuna in Belize, 1858-1969». *Ethnohistory*, 39 (1), 1-19.

Myers, Robert A. (1984). «Island Carib Cannibalism». *New West Indian Guide*, 3-4, 147-183.

Nickerson, Virginia and Noreen White (eds.) (1996). *The Natural Resources of the Garifuna of Orinoco*. Gays Mills, Wisconsin: Orangutan Press.

Osgood, Cornelius (1942). «Anthropology.-Prehistoric Contact between South America and the West Indies». *Proceedings of the National Academy of Sciences*, 28 (1), 1-4.

Palacio, Joseph O. (1987). «Black Carib History up to 1795» in Lita Hunter Krohn (ed.) *Readings in Belizean History, 2nd edition*. Belize City: St. John's College Press, pp. 111-119.

Palacio, Joseph O. (1995). «Aboriginal Peoples: Their Struggles with Cultural Identity in the Caricom Region». *Bulletin of Eastern Caribbean Affairs*, 20 (4), 25-40.

Palacio, Joseph O. (1997). «Gulisi. A Daughter of the Paramount Chief Joseph Chatoyer». *Belize Historical Society Newsletter*, (May/June)

Palacio, Joseph O. (2002). «Ecosystems and Social Actors: Comparative Results» in IDRC-CBCRM (ed.) *Balancing People and Resources – Interdisciplinary Research and Coastal Areas Management in the Wider Caribbean*. Heredia, Costa Rica: Editorial Fundacion UNA, pp. 483-498.

Pastor Fasquelle, Rodolfo (1998). «Historia e Identidad de los Garífunas sobre la Ubicación Simbólica de Yarumal». *Astrolabio*, 2, 14-20.

Rey, Nicolas (2001). *Les ancêtres noirs révolutionnaires dans la Ville Caribéenne d'Aujourd'hui: l'Exemple de Livingston, Guatemala.* Thèse de doctorat, Université de Paris 1.

Rey, Nicolas (2005). *Quand la Révolution, aux Amériques, était Nègre Caraibes Nöirs, Negros Franceses et autres «Oubliés» de l'Histoire.* Paris: Karthala.

Sheldon, William (1820). «Brief Account of the Caraibs who Inhabit the Antilles». *Transaction of the American Society (Archaeologia Americana),* 1, 365-433.

Taylor, Douglas MacRae (1935). «The Island Caribs of Dominica, British West Indies». *American Anthropologist,* 37 (2, Part 1), 265-272.

Taylor, Douglas MacRae (1936). «Additional Notes on the Island Caribs of Dominica, British West Indies». *American Anthropologist,* 38 (3, Part 1), 462-68.

Taylor, Douglas MacRae (1958). «Historical Implications of Linguistic Data on the Foods of the Island Carib and Black Carib». *Actas del 33rd Congreso Internacional de Americanistas, tomo 1,* 295-308.

Thomas, Leon (1953). «La Dominique et les Derniers Caraibes Insulaires». *Les Cahiers d'Outre Mer,* 6 (21), 37-60.

Thompson, Vincent Bakpetu (1987). *The Making of the African Diaspora in the Americas 1441-1900.* London: Longman.

Whitehead, Neil L. (1984). «Carib Cannibalism. The Historical Evidence». *Journal of the Society of Americanists,* 70, 69-88.

Geography / Geographie / Geografía

Bliss, Elaine (1989). *Women in Tropical Agriculture: A Case Study of the Garifuna (Black Carib) in Hopkins, Belize*. M.A. Thesis, University of Wisconsin, Milwaukee.

Colindres, Clarence Oliver Gonzales (2006). *Description and Analysis of the White Shrimp (*Litopenaeus schmitti*) Fisheries in Pearl Lagoon, Atlantic Coast of Nicaragua, with Focus on the Gear Selectivity in the Artesanal Fleets*. M.A. Thesis, Universitetet i Tromsø.

Craig, Alan K. (1966). *Geography of Fishing in British Honduras and Adjacent Coastal Waters*. Baton Rouge: Louisiana State University Press.

Davidson, William V. (1974). *Historical Geography of the Bay Islands, Honduras*. Birmingham, Alabama: Southern University Press.

Davidson, William V. (1976). «Black Carib (Garifuna) Habitats in Central America» in Mary W. Helms and Franklin O. Loveland (ed.) *Frontier Adaptations in Lower Central America*. Philadelphia: Institute for the Study of Human Issues, pp. 85-94.

Davidson, William V. (1976). «Coastal Imperative Lost? Village Abandonment among the Honduran Garifuna». *Actes du XLIIe Congres International des Americanistes*, 6, 571-576.

Davidson, William V. (1976). «Dispersal of the Garifuna in the Western Caribbean». *Actes du XLIIe Congres International des Americanistes*, 6, 467-474.

Davidson, William V. (1977). «Research in Coastal Ethnogeography: The East Coast of Central America». *Geoscience and Man*, XVIII, 277-284.

Davidson, William V. and Melanie A. Counce (1989). «Mapping the Distribution of Indians in Central America». *Cultural Survival*, 13 (3), 37-40.

Dixon, C.V. (1981). *Coconuts and Man on the North Coast of Honduras: An Historical Geographical Perspective*. M.A. Thesis, Louisiana State University.

Dixon, C.V. (1981). «Coconuts and Man on the North Coast of Honduras» <http://sites.maxwell.syr.edu/CLAG/year-book1985/dixon.pdf> viewed 3 February 2011.

Fewkes, J. Walter (1914). «Relations of Aboriginal Culture and Environment in the Lesser Antilles». *Bulletin of the American Geographical Society,* 46 (9), 662-678.

Lansing, David (2009). «The Spaces of Social Capital: Livelihood Geographies and Marine Conservation in the Cayos Cochinos Marine Protected Area, Honduras». *Journal of Latin American Geography,* 8 (1), 29-54.

Lundberg, Paul Arthur (1978). *Barranco: A Sketch of a Belizean Garifuna (Black Carib) Habitat.* MS in Geography at the University of California at Riverside.

Mack, Taylor (1997). *Ephemeral Hinterlands and the Historical Geography of Trujillo, Honduras, 1525-1950.* Ph.D. Thesis, Louisiana State University.

Neveu-Lemaire, M. (1921). «Les Caraibes des Antilles: Leurs Representants Actuels dans l'Ile de la Dominique». *La Geographie,* 35 (January-May), 127-146.

Potter, Robert B. (1992). «Demographic Change in a Small Island State: St. Vincent and the Grenadines, 1980-1991». *Geography,* 77 (Part 4, No. 337), 374-376.

Reclus, Elisee (1891). *The Earth and its Inhabitants. North America. Vol II.* New York: D. Appleton and Co.

Health and Medicine / Santé et Medecine/ Salud y Medicina

Alvarez, Berta and Edgar Monterroso, Gabriela Paz-Bailey, Sonia Morales-Miranda, et al. (2009). «High Rates of STD and Sexual Risk Behaviors Among Garifunas in Honduras». *Journal of Acquired Immune Deficiency Syndromes,* 51 (May), 26-34.

Barrett, Bruce (1992). *The Syringe and the Rooster Dance: Medical Anthropology on Nicaragua's Atlantic Coast.* Ph.D. Thesis, University of Wisconsin, Madison.

Barrett, Bruce (1994). «Medicinal Plants of Nicaragua's Atlantic Coast». *Economic Botany,* 48 (1), 8-20.

Barrett, Bruce (1995). «Ethnomedical Interactions: Health and Identity on Nicaragua's Atlantic Coast». *Social Science and Medicine,* 40 (12), 1611-1621.

Brady, Scott Arlen (1990). *The Nutritional Status of the Hopkins, Belize Garifuna.* M.A. Thesis, Louisiana State University.

Castillo, Gloria (2002). *Factores Sociales y Culturales Asociados a la Prevalencia de VIH/SIDA en la Población Garifuna de Guatemala,.* Master's of Public Health Thesis, Universidad de San Carlos, Guatemala.

Cayetano, Felene (2005). *Garifuna Elder Care.* Honors project, University of Baltimore.

Coe, Felix Gilmore (1995). *Ethnobotany of the Garifuna of Eastern Nicaragua.* Ph.D. Thesis, University of Connecticut.

Coe, Felix Gilmore and Gregory J. Anderson (1996). «Ethnobotany of the Garifuna of Eastern Nicaragua». *Economic Botany,* 50 (1), 71-107.

Cohen, Milton (1984). «The Ethnomedicine of the Garifuna (Black Carib) of Rio Tinto, Honduras». *Anthropological Quarterly,* 57 (1), 16-27.

Cohen, Florence S. (1979). «El Parto y el Rol de Comadrona en una Aldea Garifuna de Honduras». *Yaxkin,* 3 (1), 27-46.

Cohen, Florence S, (1982). «Childbirth Belief and Practice in a Garifuna (Black Carib) Village on the North Coast of Honduras». *Western Journal of Nursing Research,* 4 (2), 193-208.

Cosminsky, Sheila (1976). «Birth Rituals and Symbolism:A Quiche Maya-Black Carib Comparison» in P. Young and J. Howe (ed.) *Ritual and Symbol in Native Central America.* Eugene: Dept. of Anthropology, University of Oregon, pp. 105-123.

Cosminsky, Shelia (1976). «Medicinal Plants of the Black Caribs. «. *Actes du XLIIe Congres International des Americanistes,* 6, 535-552.

Dobson, Narda (1973). *A History of Belize.* Port of Spain, Trinidad and Tobago: Longman Caribbean.

Grieb, Suzanne Michelle Dolwick (2009). *Gender, Transnational Migration, and HIV Risk Among the Garinagu of Honduras and New York City.* Ph.D. Thesis, University of Florida.

Guertin, M. (2003). *La Conservation et les Mesures de Protection des Plantes Médicinales Utilisées par le Peuple Garifuna de Livingston, au Guatemala.* Ensayo de Maestria, Université de Sherbrooke.

Herrera-Paz, E. F. (2008). «Allele Frequencies Distributions for 13 Autosomal STR loci in 3 Black Carib (Garifuna) Populations of the Honduran Caribbean Coasts». *Forensic Science International Genetics,* 3 (1), 5-10.

Herrera-Paz, E.F. (2010). «The Garifuna (Black Carib) People of the Atlantic Coasts of Honduras: Population Dynamics, Structure, and Phylogenetic Relations Inferred from Genetic Data, Migration Matrices, and Isonymy». *American Journal of Human Biology,* 22 (1), 36-44.

Hutchinson, Janice (1984). *A Biocultural Analysis of Blood Pressure Variation among the Black Caribs and Creoles of St. Vincent, West Indies.* Ph.D. Thesis, University of Kansas.

Hutchinson, Janis (1986). «Association Between Stress and Blood Pressure Variation in a Caribbean Population». *American Journal of Physical Anthropology,* 71, 69-79.

Hutchinson, Janis and Pamela J. Byard (1987). «Family Resemblance for Anthropometric and Blood Pressure Measurements in Black Caribs and Creoles from St. Vincent Island». *American Journal of Physical Anthropology*, 73, 33-39.

Jenkins, Carol L. (1980). *Patterns of Protein-Energy Malnutrition among Preschoolers in Belize.* Ph.D. Thesis, University of Tennessee, Knoxville.

Jenkins, Carol L. (1981). «Patterns of Growth and Malnutrition among Preschoolers in Belize». *American Journal of Physical Anthropology*, 56, 169-178.

Jenkins, Carol L (1984). «Nutrition and Growth in Early Childhood among the Garifuna and Creole of Belize» in Michael H. Crawford (ed.) *Current Developments in Anthropological Genetics. Vol. 3: Black Caribs: A Case Study in Biocultural Adaptation.* New York: Plenum Press, pp. 135-147.

Palacio, Joseph O. (1994). «Health Conditions of Aboriginal Peoples in Belize, Guyana and Suriname» prepared for PAO, Washington.

Perez Valenzuela, Pedro (1956). *Santo Tomas: Apuntes para la Historia de las Colonizaciones en la Costa Atlantica.* Guatemala: Tipografio. Nacional.

Poll, Elfriede de and C. Mejia and M. Szejner (2005). *Etnobotanica Garifuna: Livingston, Izabal, Guatemala.* Guatemala: Universidad del Valle de Guatemala, Departamento de Biologia.

Shavender, Kimberly M. (1996). *Choice of Medical Care in a Pluralistic Medical System: Punta Gorda, Belize.* M.S. in Public Health Thesis, The University of Colorado.

Simmons, Jennifer Louise (2008). *Gender, Sexuality and HIV Risk in Belize: A Mixed Method Study.* Ph.D. Thesis, University of California, Los Angeles.

Stansbury, James P. (2004). «Risks, Stigma and Honduran Garifuna Conceptions of HIV/AIDS». *Social Science and Medicine*, 59 (3), 457-471.

Stein, Renee W. (1996). «Among the Garifuna in Central America». *Midwifery Today and Childbirth Education*, 7, 17.

Stupp, Paul W. and Beth A. Macke, Richard Monteith and Sandra Paredez (1994). «Ethnicity and the Use of Health Services in Belize». *Journal of Biosocial Science,* 26 (2), 165-177.

Tejada, Carlos and Nancie Gonzalez and Margarita Sanchez (1965). «El Factor Diego y el Gene de Celulas Falciformes entre los Caribes de Raza Negra do Livingston, Guatemala». *Revista del Colegio Medico de Guatemala,* 16 (2), 83-86.

Weymes, H.M. (1979). *Variant Haemoglobins and other Inherited Blood Factors in the Black Carib Community of Central America.* Ph.D. Thesis, University of London.

Weymes, Hazel and Henry Gershowitz (1984). «Genetic Structure of the Garifuna Population in Belize» in Michael H. Crawford (ed.) *Current Developments in Anthropological Genetics. Vol. 3: Black Caribs: A Case Study in Biocultural Adaptation.* New York: Plenum Press, pp. 271-287.

History / Histoire / Historia

Abbot, Eliner (1966). *Black Caribs, Belizean Nationalism, and the Carib Development Society in Stann Creek, British Honduras* prepared for Anthropology Department of Brandeis University.

Adams, Edgar (2002). *People on the Move: The Effects of Some Important Historical Events on the People of St. Vincent and the Grenadines.* Kingstown, St. Vincent and the Grenadines: Rand M. Adams Book Centre.

Alegria, R.E. (1978). «The Use of Noxious Gas in Warfare by the Taino and Carib Indians of the Antilles». *Revista/Review Interamericana,* 8 (3), 409-15.

Arana, Frank (1996). «It Used to Be That... A Garifuna Belorio (nine night) was interesting and Exciting». *Amandala,* 13 (7 Jan), 17.

Arana, Frank (1997). *It Used to Be That...* Belize: National Printers Ltda.

Arrivillaga Cortés, Alfonso (2005). «Marcos Sanchez Diaz: From Hero to Hiuraha: Two Hundred Years of Garifuna Settlement in Central America» in Joseph O. Palacio (ed.) *The Garífuna, a Nation Across Borders: Essays in Social Anthropology.* Belize: Cubola Press, pp. 64-84.

Atwood, Thomas (1791). *History of the Island of Dominica.* London: J. Johnson.

Bagneris, Amanda Michaela (2009). *Coloring the Caribbean: Agostino Brunias and the Painting of Race in the British West Indies, c.1765-1800.* Ph.D. Thesis, Harvard University.

Beaucage, Pierre and Marcel Samson (1964). *Historia del Pueblo Garifuna y su Llegada a Honduras en 1796.* Honduras: Patronato para el Desarrollo de las Comunidades de los Departamentos de Colón y Gracias a Dios.

Beckles, Hilary McD. (1992). «Kalinago(Carib) Resistance to European Colonisation of the Caribbean». *Caribbean Quarterly,* 38 (2-3), 1-14.

Bell, C. Napier (1899). *Tangweera: Life and Adventures among Gentle Savages.* London: Edward Arnold.

Bendaña Perdomo, Ricardo (2006). «La Compañía de Jesús en Guatemala Siglo XIX». *Anales de la Academia de Geografía e Historia de Guatemala,* 169-212.

Blondeel Van Cuelebrouk, M. (1846). *Colonie de SantoTomas.* Brussels: Le Ministre des Affaires Etrangeres.

Bolland, O. Nigel (1977). *The Formation of a Colonial Society: Belize from Conquest to Crown Colony.* Baltimore: Johns Hopkins University Press.

Bradley, Leo (1987). «Carib Villages of Belize» in Lita Hunter Krohn (ed.) *Readings in Belizean History, 2nd edition.* Belize City: Belizean Studies, pp. 120-121.

Bridge, William S. (1900). *Roseau: Reminiscences of Life as I Found it in the Island of Dominica, and among the Carib Indians.* New York: Isaac H. Blanchard.

Bristowe, Lindsay W. and Philip B. Wright (1888). *The Handbook of British Honduras for 1888-89.* Edinburgh and London: William Blackwood and Sons.

Buhler, S.J., Richard (1976). *A History of the Catholic Church in Belize.* Belize City: Belize Institute for Social Research and Action.

Campbell, Susan (2001). «Defending Aboriginal Sovereignty: The 1930 'Carib War' in Waitukubuli (Dominica)» <http:// www.cavehill.uwi.edu/BNCCde/dominica/conference/ Papers/CampbellS.html viewed 3 February 2011>.

Cardenas Ruiz, Manuel (1981). *Cronicas Francesas de los Indios Caribes.* Rio Piedras, Puerto Rico: Editorial Universidad de Puerto Rico.

Carr, Archie (1953). *High Jungles and Low.* Gainesville: University of Florida Press.

Cayetano, Sebastian (1997). *Garifuna history, language and cultura of Belize, Central America and the Caribbean. Bicentennial Edition (April 12 1797 - April 12 1997).* Belize: BRC.

Centeno García, Santos (1996). *Historia del Pueblo Negro Caribe y su Llegada a Hibueras el 12 de Abril de 1797.* Tegucigalpa, Honduras: Universidad Nacional Autónoma de Honduras, Editorial Universitaria.

Centeno Garcia, Santos (1997). *Historia del Movimiento Negro Hondureño*. Tegucigalpa: Editorial Guaymuras.

Charles, Cecil (1890). *Honduras: The Land of Great Depths*. Chicago and New York: Rand McNally and Company.

Cleghorn, Robert (1939). *A Short History of Baptist Missionary Work in British Honduras*. London: Kingsgate Press, p. 71.

Craton, Michael (1982). *Testing the Chains Resistance to Slavery in the British West Indies*. Ithaca: Cornell University Press, p. 389.

Craton, Michael (1986). «From Caribs to Black Caribs: The Amerindian Roots of Servile Resistance in the Caribbean» in Okihiro, Gary Y. (ed.) *Resistance Studies in African, Caribbean, and Afro-American History*. Amherst: The University of Massachusetts Press, pp. 96-116.

Douglas, James (1869). «Account of the Attempt to Form a Settlement on the Mosquito Shore, in 1823». *Transactions of the Literary Society of Quebec*, Series 2, Vol. 6 (6-7), 25-39.

Du Tertre, Jean-Baptiste (1654). *Histoire Générale des Isles de S. Christophe, de la Guadeloupe, de la Martinique et autres dans l'Amérique*. Paris.

Duron, Romulo Ernesto (1927). *Bosquejo de la Historia de Honduras*. San Pedro Sula: Tip. del Comercio, p. 216.

Ellis, Godsman (1997). *The Garinagu of Belize*. San Ignacio: The Haman Belize.

Fabel, Robin F. A. (2000). *Colonial Challenges: Britons, Native Americans, and Caribs, 1759-1775*. Gainesville: University of Florida Press.

Flores, Justo (1979). *The Garifuna Story Now and Then*. Los Angeles: self published.

Flores, Justo (1993). *The Garifuna Story Now and Then Book Two*. Los Angeles: self published.

Flores, Justo (1995). *Life and Obituary of Aunt Dominica – A Bilingual Garifuna Story*. Los Angeles: self published.

Froebel, Julius (1859). *Seven Years' Travel in Central America*. London: Richard Bentley.

Gibbs, Archibald Robertson (1883). *British Honduras: An Historical and Descriptive Account of the Colony from its Settlement, 1670*. London: Sampson Low, Marston, Searle, and Rivington.

Grant, C. H. (1976). *The Making of Modern Belize, Politics, Society and British Colonialism in Central America*. Cambridge: Cambridge University Press.

Hadel, Richard (1987). «Carib Dates» in Lita Hunter Krohn (ed.) *Readings in Belizean History, 2nd edition*. Belize City: Belizean Studies, p. 110.

Honychurch, Lennox (2002). «The Leap at Sauteurs: The Lost Cosmology of Indigenous Grenada» <http://www.cavehill. uwi.edu/BNCCde/grenada/conference/Papers/LH.html viewed 3 February 2011>.

Houdaille, Jacques (1954). «Negros Franceses en America Central a Fines del Siglo XVIII». *Antropologia e Historia de Guatemala*, 6 (1), 65-67.

Howard, Richard and Elizabeth Howard (ed.) (1983). *Alexander Anderson's Geography and History of St. Vincent, West Indies*. Cambridge: Arnold Arboretum.

Jacobs, Curtis (2003). «The Brigands's War in St. Vincent: The View from the French Records, 1794-1796» presented at the St.Vincent and the Grenadines Country Conference.

Jenkins, H. J. K. (1977). «The Colonial Robespierre: Victor Hugues on Guadeloupe 1794-98». *History Today*, 27 (11), 734-741.

Jenkins, H. J. K. (1980). «Guadeloupe 1799-1803: A Haiti Manqué». *History Today*, 30 (4), 13-16.

Jenkins, H. J. K. (1981). «Martinique: The British Occupation, 1794-1802». *History Today*, 31 (11), 35-39.

Keenagh, Peter (1938). *Mosquito Coast: An Account of a Journey Through the Jungles of Honduras*. London: Chatto and Windus.

Kirby, I. Earle and C.I. Martin (1972). *The Rise and Fall of the Black Caribs of St. Vincent*. St. Vincent: St. Vincent and the Grenadines National Trust, p. 52.

La Borde, (1674). Voyage qui Contient Une Relation Exacte des Caraibes Sauvages des Antilles de l'Amérique. Paris: Louis Billaine.

Labat, Jean Baptiste (1724). *Nouveau Voyage aux Isles de l'Amerique*, 8 Vols. Paris: Cavalier Pere.

Labat, Jean Baptiste (1984). *Nuevo Viaje a las Islas de la America*, Vol. I. *Rio Piedras.* Puerto Rico: Editorial de la Universidad de Puerto Rico.

Labat, Jean.Baptiste. (1931). *Voyages aux Isles de l'Amerique.* Paris: Editions Duchartre.

Lawrence, Harold (Kofi Wangara) (1986). «Mandinga Voyages across the Atlantic». *Journal of African Civilizations*, 8 (2), 202-247.

López Garcia, Victor Virgilio (1994). *La Bahia del Puerto del Sol y la Masacre de los Garifunas de San Juan.* Tegucigalpa: Editorial Guaymuras.

Lunardi, Federico (1946). *Honduras Maya.* San Pedro Sula, Honduras: Compania Editora de Honduras.

Martínez, Nancy (2010). «La Historia como Discurso de Identidad. La Dominación y el Arte de la Resistencia entre los Garífunas de Guatemala». Revista Pueblos y Fronteras digital, 5 (8), 60-84. <http://www.pueblosyfronteras.unam.mx/a09n8/pdfs/n8_art03.pdf> viewed 6 January 2012.

Maudsley, Anne Cary and Alfred Percival Maudslay (1899). *A Glimpse at Guatemala and Some Notes on the Ancient Monuments of Central America.* London: John Murray, Reissued by Cambridge University Press, 2010.

Moreau, Jean-Pierre (2002). *Un Flibustier Francais dans la Mer des Antilles (1618-1620).* Paris: Editions Payot and Rivages.

Muilenburg, Peter T. (1992). «Sea Kings of the Antilles». *Americas,* 44 (July), 16-21.

Muilenburg, Peter T. (1999). «Black Carib Bastion of Freedom». *Americas,* 51 (May), 16-21.

Ober, Frederick A. (1880). *Camps in the Caribbees: The Adventures of a Naturalist in the Lesser Antilles.* Boston: Lee and Shepard.

Ober, Frederick A. (1895). «Aborigines of the West Indies». *Proceedings of the American Antiquariam*, 9, 270-313.

Ober, Frederick A. (1906). *Juan Ponce de Leon*. New York: Harper and Brothers.

Ober, Frederick A. (1912). *Our West Indian Neighbors*. New York: James Pott and Company.

Ober, Frederick A. (1928). *A Guide to the West Indies, Bermuda and Panama*. New York: Dodd, Mead and Company.

Palacio, Joseph O. (1973). «Black Carib History Up to 1795». *Journal of Belizean Affairs*, 1, 31-41.

Palacio, Myrtle (1993). *The First Primer on the People Called the Garifuna: The Things You Have Always Wanted to Know!* Belize City: Glessima Research and Services.

Payne Iglesias, Elizet (2008). «Presentación del Padrón de Truxillo de 1821». Boletin AFEHC, 38 <http://afehc-historia-centroamericana.org/index.php?action=fi_affandid=2046> viewed 14 January 2011.

Pim, Bedford (1869). *Dotting on the Roadside in Panama, Nicaragua et Mosquito*. London: Chapman and Hall, p. 468.

Plas O.S.B., D. Gualbert van der (1954). *The History of the Massacre of Two Jesuit Missionaries in the Island of St. Vincent 24th January, 1654*. Kingstown GP: government publication.

Porter, Robert William III (1984). *History and Social Life of the Garifuna in the Lesser Antilles and Central America*. Ph.D. Thesis, Princeton University.

Ramos, Adele (2000). *Thomas Vincent Ramos: The Man and His Writings*. Dangriga, Belize: National Garifuna Council.

Raynal, Guillame Thomas Francoise (1798). *A Philosophical and Political History of the Settlements and Trade of the Europeans in the East and West Indies. 6 Vol.* London: W. Strahan.

Rey, Nicolas (2006). «Caribes Noirs et "Negros Franceses" (Caraibes/Antilles): Le Périple des Noirs Révolutionnaires» in Carmen Bernand, Alessandro Stella (ed.), *D'esclaves à Soldats. Miliciiens et Soldats d'Origine Servile. XII –XXI siècles*. Paris : L'Harmattan, pp. 201-217.

Rey, Nicolas (2006). «Les Chefs de la Révolution Haïtienne en Exil, de Saint-Domingue à l'Amérique Centrale» in Bonacci, Giulia, Dimitri Béchacq, Pascale Berloquin-Chassany, y Nicolas Rey (ed.) *La Révolution Haïtienne au-delà de ses Frontières*. Paris: Karthala.

Rubio Sánchez, Manuel (1975). *Historia del Puerto de Trujillo, tomos I y II*. Tegucigalpa: Banco Central de Honduras.

Sanborn, Helen J. (1886). *A Winter in Central America and Mexico*. Boston: Lee and Shepard Publishers.

Shephard, Charles (1971). *An Historical Account of the Island of Saint Vincent*. London: Frank Cass and Company Limited.

Squire, E.G. (1855). *Notes on Central America*. New York: Harper.

Squier, E.G. (1856). *Apuntamientos sobre Centroamérica, particularmente sobre los Estados de Honduras y San Salvador*. Paris: Imprenta de G. Gratios.

Squier, E. George (1891). *Adventures on the Mosquito Shore*. New York: Worthington Co.

Stephens, John L. (1969). *Incidents of Travel in Central America, Chiapas Yucatan Vol. I*. New York: Dover Publications.

Suazo, Salvador (1997). *Los Deportados de San Vincente*. Tegucigalpa: Editorial Guaymuras.

Suazo, Salvador (2008). «Catarino Castro Serrano: Primer Intellectual Garfíuna Hondureño. Apuntes Bibliográficos». *Yaxkin*, 24 (1), 109-111.

Sweeney, James L. (2005). *History as National Myth: The War of the Brigands or the Second Carib War. A Story of Vincentian Nationalism*. M. A. Thesis, California State University, Dominguez Hills.

Swett, Charles (1868). *A Trip to British Honduras and to San Pedro, Republic of Honduras*. New Orleans: Price Current Print.

Thomas, J. Paul (1984). «The Caribs of St. Vincent: A Study in Imperial Maladministration 1763-73». *Journal of Caribbean History*, 18 (2), 60-73.

Wallstrom, Tord (1955). *A Wayfarer in Central America*. New York: Roy Publishers.

West, Phil (1993). *The Sandinista Revolutionary Project on the Atlantic Coast, 1979-90: Conflict and Reconciliation in the Context of Inter-cultural Conflict and US Destabilisation*. Thesis, La Trope University.

Young, William (1971). *An Account of the Black Charaibs in the Island of St. Vincents*. London: Frank Cass and Co.

Language and Linguistics / Langage et Linguistique / Lenguaje y Lingüística

Adam, Lucien (1893). Matériaux pour Servir à l'Etablissement d'une Grammaire Compare des Dialectes de la Famille Caribe. Paris: Ed. J Maisonneuve, p. 139.

Adam, Lucien (1904). «Le Caraibe du Honduras et Le Caraibe des Iles». *Internationales Amerik Kongress (ICA)*, 14, 357-371.

Adam, Lucien (1940). «Lengua Caribe. Del Hablar de los Hombres y del Hablar de las Mujeres en la Lengua Caribe». *Revista Nacional de Cultura*, 11 (21), 16-30.

Allsopp, Richard (1965). «British Honduras: The Linguistic Dilemma». *Caribbean Quarterly*, 11 (3), 54-64.

Arzu, W. M. (1986). «A Logical Chronology of Months' Names in Garifuna Carib». *Belizean Studies*, 14 (5-5), 29-39.

Berendt, C. H. (1873). «On a Grammer and Dicionary of the Carib or Karif Language, with some Account of the People by Whom it is Spoke». *Smithsonian Institute Annual Report*.

Bertilson, Kathryn (1989). *Introduccion al Idioma Garifuna: Recopilado y escrito por Kathryn Bertilson con la Colaboracion de la Direccion General de Alfabetizacion y Educacion de Adultos.* Tegucigalpa: Cuerpo de Paz Honduras, Sector de Educacion No-Formal: Ministerio de Educacion Pública.

Bonner, Donna Maria (2001). «Garifuna Children's Language Shame: Ethnic Stereotypes, National Affiliation and Transnational Immigration as Factors in Language Choice in Belize». *Language in Society*, 30 (1), 81-96.

Breton, Raymond (1665). *La Dictionnaire Caraïbe-Française.* Auxerre, France: Gilles Bouquet.

Breton, Raymond (1958). *Carib-French Dictionary: Father Breton's Observations of the Island Carib, A Compilation of Ethnographic Notes (1665).* New Haven: Human Relation Area Files.

Breton, Raymond 1665, édité par Marina Besada Paisa *et al.* (1999). *Dictionnaire Caraïbe-Français.* Paris: IRD/Karthala.

Breton, Raymond (1667). *Grammaire Caraibe.* Auxerre, France: Gilles Bouquet.

Breton, Raymond (1877). *Grammaire Caraibe, Catéchisme Caraibe, Nouvelle edition.* Paris: L'Adam and Charles Le Clerc.

Breton, Raymond (1968). *Grammaire Caraibe suivie du Catechisme Caraibe.* Nendeln, Liechtenstein: Kraus Reprint.

Castillo Mathieu, Nicolás del (1975). *Léxico Caribe en el Caribe Negro de Honduras Británica.* Bogotá: Instituto Caro y Cuervo.

Cayetano, E. Roy (1998). «La Experiencia de la Lengua Garífuna» in Ramos McNab (ed.) *Primer Eje: Educación Bilingüe Intercultural.* Tegucigalpa: El Taller.

Cayetano, Roy (ed.) (1993). *The People's Garifuna Dictionary: Dimureiágei Garifuna.* Dangriga: The National Garifuna Council of Belize.

Cayetano, E. Roy (1981). *Writing Garifuna: Towards a Common Garifuna Orthography.* Belize.

Conzemius, Eduard (1999). «Material Sobre el Idioma Garif (Honduras)». *Yaxkin,* 18 (1), 80-116.

de Pury, Sybille (2000). «Les Verbes Empruntés au Français par le Garifuna: des Verbes d'Etat?». *Amerindia,* 25, 49-64.

de Pury, Sybille (2002). «Quand les Langues Réagissent». *Cahiers Critiques de Thérapie Familiale et de Pratiques de Réseaux,* 2 (29), 239-249.

de Pury, Sybille (2001). «Le Garifuna, une Langue Mixte». *Faits de Langues,* 18, 75-84.

de Pury, Sybille (2003). «Vice Versa. Le Genre en Garifuna». *Faits de Langues,* 21, 155-162.

de Pury Toumi, Sybille and Marcella Lewis (2001). The Language of the Callinago People, Father Breton's Dictionnaire Caraibe-Francais (1665) Compared with Garifuna. <http://www.sup-infor.com/navigation.htm> viewed 3 February 2011.

de Pury Toumi, Sybille (1995). «Flibusterie et Evangelisation dans les Petites Antilles au debut de la Colonisation: Ni Dieu, ni Diable». *Amerindia,* 19/20, 351-362.

de Pury Toumi, Sybille (1991). «Lorsque Beau-Frere Devient Belle-Soeur: Analyse de un Cas de Contact Linguistique». *Nouvelle Revue d'Ethnopsychiatrie,* 17, 111-123.

Devonish, Hubert and Enita Castillo (2002). «On the Interface Between Morphology and Syntax: Simple and Complex Sentences in Garifuna» presented to 14th Biennial Conference, Society for Caribbean Language and Linguistics, St. Augustine, Trinidad andTobago, August, 2002.

Drom, Elaine (2004). *A Semantic Sketch of Spacial Grams in Garifuna.* M.A. Thesis, San Jose State University.

Escure, Genevieve (1979). «Linguistic Variation and Ethnic Interaction in Belize: Creole/Carib» in Howard Giles and Bernard Saint-Jacques (ed.) *Language and Ethnic Relations.* Oxford: Pergamon Press, pp. 101-116.

Escure, Genevieve (1983). «The Use of Creole as Interlanguage by the Black Carib of Belize» in Ingemann, Frances (ed.) *1982 Mid-America Language and Linguistics Conference papers.* Lawrence: Department of Language and Linguistics, The University of Kansas, pp. 271-282.

Escure, Genevieve (1983). «Contrastive Patterns of Intragroup and Intergroup Interaction in the Creole Continum of Belize». *Language in Society,* 11, 239-264.

Escure, Genevieve (1984). «The Acquisition of Creole by Urban and Rural Black Caribs in Belize» in Mark Sebba and Loreto Todd (ed.) *York Papers in Language and Linguistics 11: Urban Creoles,* , 95-104.

Escure, Geneviève (1991). «De l'Usage du Créole par les Mayas et les Afro-Indiens du Bélize». *Etudes Créoles,* 14 (2), 114-128.

Escure, Genevieve (1993). «Focus and Grammatical Relations in Creole Languages» in Francis Byrne, Donald Winford (ed.) *Creole Language Library.* Amsterdam/Philadelphia: John Benjamins Publishing Company, pp. 233-247.

Escure, Geneviève (2004). «Garifuna in Belize and Honduras» in Geneviève Escure and Arm in Schwegler (ed.) *Creoles, Contact and Language Change: Linguistic and Social Implications.*

Amsterdam and Philadelphia: John Benjamins Publishing Company, pp. 35-66.

Flores, Justo (1983). *A Study of the Reading and Writing of Garifuna - Garifuna, English, Spanish.* Los Angeles: self published.

Flores, Justo (1990). *The History of the Writing of Garifuna in our Time: Say It as You See It.* Los Angeles: self published.

Flores, Justo (1992). *Now or Never - To the Future of the Garifuna Language.* Los Angeles: self published.

Flores, Justo (1994). *Bilingual Garifuna Study.* Los Angeles: self published.

Goeje, C.H. De (1939). «Nouvel Examen des Langues des Antilles». *Societe des Americanistes,* 31, 1-120.

Guevara, Martha (2002). «Relato de Migracion Garifuna» <http://martha.guevara.free.fr/2_relato.pdf> viewed 3 February 2011.

Hadel, Richard and J. J. Stochl, and Roman Zuniga (1975). *A Dictionary of Central American Carib.* Belize City: BISRA.

Hadel, Richard (1976). «Reflections on Garifuna Language and Society». *Actes du XLIIe Congres International des Americanistes,* 6, 475-486.

Hagiwara, Robert (1993). «Predictability in Garifuna Vowel Alternations: A problem for Radical Underspecification». *UCLA Occasional Papers in Language and Linguistics,* (13), 49-59.

Harvey, Jennifer (1995). «The Garifuna Language in Barranco: A Need for Preservation» Vermont Paper for School for International Training.

Henderson, Alexander (1872). Grammar an Dictonary of the Karif Language of Honduras (fron Belize ti Little Rock). 8 Vol <http://collections.si.edu/search/results.jsp?q=record_ID:siris_arc_82969> viewed 15 December 2011.

Holmes, Keith R. (1987). *Verb Structure of Central American Garifuna Language.* M.A. Thesis, Louisaiana State University.

Jamieson, Mark (1998). «Linguistic Innovation and Relationship Terminology in the Pearl Lagoon Basin of

Nicaragua». *Journal of the Royal Anthropological Institute,* 4 (4), 713-730.

LePage, Robert (1992). «You can never tell where a word comes from: Language Contact in a Diffuse Setting» in Ernst Jahr (ed.) *Language Contact: Theoretical and Empirical Studies.* Berlin: Mouton de Gruyter, pp. 71-101.

Martinez Cayetano, Mateo (2001). *Daradu Luagu Labüriidüniwa Garífuna, Laminda Meriga = Normas de Escritura de la Lengua Garífuna/ Sistematización.* Tegucigalpa: Proyecto Mejoramiento de la Calidad de la Educación Básica.

Prescod, Paula (2008). «A Demolinguistic Profile of St. Vincent and the Grenadines or a Successful Attempt at Linguistic Disenfranchisement». *Anthropos,* 103 (1), 99-112.

Rat, Joseph Numa (1898). «The Carib Language as now Spoken in Dominica, West Indies». *Journal of the Anthropological Institute of Great Britian and Ireland,* 27 (2), 293-315.

Ravindranath, Maya (2009). *Language Shift and the Speech Community: Sociolinguistic Change in a Garifuna Community in Belize.* Ph.D. Thesis, University of Pennsylvania.

Reyes, David Wahayona Campos (2004). «The Origin and Survival of the Taino Language». Issues in Caribbean Amerindian Studies, 5 (2) <http://www.centrelink.org/davidcampos.html>. viewed 3 February 2011.

Rivera y Morillo, Humberto (1977). *Diccionario Garífuna.* San Pedro Sula, Honduras: CURN.

Shafer, Robert (1963). «Verglichende Phonetik der Karaibischen Sprachen». *Verhandelingen der Koninlijke Nederlandse Akademie van Wetenschappen, AFD. Letterkunde,* 69 (2), 4-78.

Suazo, Salvador (1991). *Conversamos en Garifuna: Grámatica y Manual de Conversación.* Tegucigalpa, Honduras: COPRODEIM.

Suazo, Salvador (2000). *La Escritura Garífuna = Abürühani lau Garifuna.* Tegucigalpa: CEDEC/CORDAID.

Suazo, Salvador and Duna Troiani, Sybille Toumi (2001). «De Caribe a Garifuna, un Estudio Comparativo de la Lengua

Caribe del Siglo XVII y del Garifuna Actual». *Chantiers Amerindia*, 25 (Supplement1), 39.

Taylor, Douglas MacRae (1945). «Certain Carib Morphological Influences on Creole». *International Journal of American Language and Linguistics*, 11 (3), 140-155.

Taylor, Douglas MacRae (1946). «Loan Words in Dominica Island Carib». *International Journal of American Language and Linguistics*, 12 (4), 213-216.

Taylor, Douglas MacRae (1948). «Conversations and Letter from the Black Carib of British Honduras». *International Journal of American Language and Linguistics*, 14 (2), 99-107.

Taylor, Douglas MacRae (1951). «Inflexional System of Island Carib». *International Journal of American Language and Linguistics*, 17 (1), 23-31.

Taylor, Douglas MacRae (1951). «Sex Gender in Central American Carib». *International Journal of American Language and Linguistics*, 17 (2), 102-104.

Taylor, Douglas MacRae (1951). «Morphophonemics of Island Carib (Central American Dialect)». *International Journal of American Language and Linguistics*, 17 (4), 224-234.

Taylor, Douglas MacRae (1952). «The Principal Grammatical Formatives of Island Carib (C. A. Dialect)». *International Journal of American Language and Linguistics*, 18 (3), 150-165.

Taylor, Douglas MacRae (1952). «Sameness and Difference in Two Island Carib Dialects». *International Journal of American Language and Linguistics*, 18 (4), 223-230.

Taylor, Douglas MacRae (1953). «A Note on the Identification of Some Island Carib Suffixes». *International Journal of American Language and Linguistics*, 19 (3), 195-200.

Taylor, Douglas MacRae (1953). «A Note on Some Arawak-Carib Lexical Resemblance». *International Journal of American Language and Linguistics*, 19 (4), 316-317.

Taylor, Douglas MacRae (1954). «Diachronic Note on the Carib Contribution to Island Carib». *International Journal of American Language and Linguistics*, 20 (1), 28-33.

Taylor, Douglas MacRae (1954). «A Note on the Arawakan Affiliation of Taino». *International Journal of American Language and Linguistics*, 20 (2), 152-154.

Taylor, Douglas MacRae and Irving Rouse (1955). «Linguistic and Archeological Time Depth in the West Indies». *International Journal of American Language and Linguistics*, 21 (2), 105-115.

Taylor, Douglas MacRae (1955). «Phonemes of the Hopkins (British Honduras) Dialect of Island Carib». *International Journal of American Language and Linguistics*, 21 (3), 233-241.

Taylor, Douglas MacRae (1956). «Island Carib II: Word-Classes, Affixes, Nouns, and Verbs». *International Journal of American Language and Linguistics*, 22 (1), 1-44.

Taylor, Douglas MacRae (1956). «Island Carib Morphology III: Locators and Particles». *International Journal of American Language and Linguistics*, 22 (2), 138-150.

Taylor, Douglas MacRae (1956). «Language Contacts in the West Indies». *Word*, 12, 399-414.

Taylor, Douglas MacRae (1956). «Languages and Ghost-Languages of the West Indies». *International Journal of American Language and Linguistics*, 22 (2), 180-183.

Taylor, Douglas MacRae (1957). «Languages and Ghost-Languages of the West Indies: A Postscript». *International Journal of American Language and Linguistics*, 23 (2), 114-116.

Taylor, Douglas MacRae (1957). «On the Affiliation of Island Carib». *International Journal of American Language and Linguistics*, 23 (4), 297-302.

Taylor, Douglas MacRae (1958). «Compounds and Comparison». *International Journal of American Language and Linguistics*, 24 (1), 77-79.

Taylor, Douglas MacRae (1958). «Island Carib IV: Syntactic Notes, Texts». *International Journal of American Language and Linguistics*, 24 (1), 36-60.

Taylor, Douglas MacRae (1958). «Carib, Caliban, Cannibal». *International Journal of American Language and Linguistics*, 24 (2), 156-157.

Taylor, Douglas MacRae (1958). «Iwana~ Yuana Iguana». *International Journal of American Language and Linguistics*, 24 (2), 157-158.

Taylor, Douglas MacRae (1958). «Use and Disuse of Languages in the West Indies». *Caribbean Quarterly*, 5 (2).

Taylor, Douglas MacRae (1958). «The Place of Island Carib Within the Arawakan Family». *International Journal of American Language and Linguistics*, 24 (2), 153-156.

Taylor, Douglas MacRae (1958). «Corrigenda to Island Carib I-IV». *International Journal of American Language and Linguistics*, 24 (4), 325-326.

Taylor, Douglas MacRae (1958). «Lines by a Black Carib». *International Journal of American Language and Linguistics*, 24 (4), 324-325.

Taylor, Douglas MacRae (1959). «On Dialectal Divergence in Island Carib». *International Journal of American Language and Linguistics*, 25 (1), 62-67.

Taylor, Douglas MacRae (1959). «Errata in Island Carib IV». *International Journal of American Language and Linguistics*, 25 (2), 137.

Taylor, Douglas MacRae (1959). «A Possible Arawak-Carib Blend». *International Journal of American Language and Linguistics*, 25 (3), 195-196.

Taylor, Douglas MacRae (1959). «Morpheme Mergers in Island Carib». *International Journal of American Language and Linguistics*, 25 (3), 190-195.

Taylor, Douglas MacRae (1960). «On the History of Island-Carib Consonantism». *International Journal of American Language and Linguistics*, 26 (2), 146-155.

Taylor, Douglas MacRae (1960). «Compounds and Comparion Again». *International Journal of American Language and Linguistics*, 26 (3), 252-256.

Taylor, Douglas MacRae (1961). «Some Particular Problems in the Application of the 100-Item Lexicostatistic Test List». *International Journal of American Language and Linguistics*, 27 (1), 30-41.

Taylor, Douglas MacRae (1961). «Arawakan for Path, Bone, Hand: A Semantic Problem of Reconstruction». *International Journal of American Language and Linguistics*, 27 (4), 365-367.

Taylor, Douglas MacRae (1961). «New Languages for Old in the West Indies». *Comparative Studies in Society and History*, 3 (3), 277-288.

Taylor, Douglas MacRae (1961). «Grandchildren Versus other Semidomesticated Animals». *International Journal of American Language and Linguistics*, 27 (4), 367-370.

Taylor, Douglas MacRae (1962). «Lexical Borrowing in Island Carib». *Romance Philology*, 16 (2), 143-152.

Taylor, Douglas MacRae (1963). «On the History of Island Carib Consonantism: A Postscript». *International Journal of American Language and Linguistics*, 29 (1), 68-71.

Taylor, Douglas MacRae (1965). «Tradition in Black Carib Kinship Terminology». *International Journal of American Language and Linguistics*, 31 (3), 286-292.

Taylor, Douglas MacRae (1977). *Languages of the West Indies*. Baltimore: John Hopkins University Press.

Taylor, Douglas MacRae and B.J. Hoff (1980). «The Linguistic Repertory of the Island-Carib in the Seventeenth Century: The Men's Language - A Carib Pidgin?». *International Journal of American Language and Linguistics*, 46 (4), 301-12.

Wright, Pamela (1986). *Language Shift and the Redefinition of Social Boundaries among the Carib of Belize*. Ph.D. Thesis, City University of New York.

Wright, Pamela (1995). «The Timely Significance of Supernatural Mothers or Exemplary Daughters: The Metonymy of Identity in History» in Jane Schneider and Rayna Rapp (ed.) *Articulating Hidden Histories*. Berkeley: University of California Press, pp. 243-261.

Literature / Littérature / Literatura

Amaya Banegas, Jorge Alberto (2007). *Las Imágenes de los Negros Garífunas en la Literatura Hondureña y Extranjera.* Tegucigalpa: Secretaría de Cultura, Artes y Deportes.

Castillo, Jesse (1994). *Garifuna Folktales.* Brooklyn, New York: Caribbean Research Center Press.

Doherty, Nelita M. (1998). *Aba Wama.* Dominican Republic: Segraf Publications.

Doherty, Nelita M. (1998). *Journey On.* Dominican Republic: Segraf Publishers.

Doherty, Nelita M. (1999). *Garinagus' Exile.* Dominican Republic: Segraf Publications.

Emery-Waterhouse, Frances (1947). *Banana Paradise.* New York: Stephen-Paul Publishers.

Flores, Justo (no date). *Gatati Le, The alcoholic, El Borracho.* Los Angeles: self published.

Flores, Justo (1977). *Tomba Le.* Los Angeles: self published.

Frederick, Faustulus J. and Elizabeth Shepherd (1971). *In our Carib Village.* New York: Lothrop, Lee and Shepard.

Hernandez, Felicia (1988). *Those Ridiculous Years: A Collection of Short Stories.* Belize City: Angelus Press.

Lee, William (1869). «Imaginary Destruction of the Isle of St. Vincent: *Daniel Defoe his Life and Recently Discovered Writings».* London: J. C. Hotten, pp. 48-55.

Lee, William (1969). *Daniel Defoe: His Life and Recently Discovered Writing Vol. II, The First Volume of his Writings.* New York: B. Franklin.

Lewis, Marcella (1994). *Walagante Marcella: Marcella Our Legacy.* Caye Caulker, Belize: Producciones de la Hamaca.

London, Jonathan (1996). *The Village Basket Weaver.* New York: Dutton Children's Books.

Morgan, Govel (1993). *Southern Children.* Belize: self published.

Morgan, Govel (1999). *Anigi Peini (Punta Gorda).* Belize: G. Morgan.

Rey, Nicolas (2009). *Crazy Caraibe*. Paris: Sarbacane.

Shaw, Mary (ed.) (1971). *According to our Ancestors*. Norman, OK: Summer Institute of Language and Linguistics.

Shaw, Mary (ed.) (1972). *Segun Nuestros Antepasados: Textos folklóricos de Guatemala y Honduras*. Guatemala: Instituto Linguistico de Verano, p. 502.

Yuscarán, Guillermo (1997). *Cuando Chona Cantaba = When Chona Sang*. Tegucigalpa: Nuevo Sol Publicaciones.

Music, Dance and Arts / Musique, Danse et Arts / Musica, Danza y Artes

AECID - Agencia Española de Cooperación para el Desarrollo, (2010). *En Clave Afrocaribe.* Guatemala: El Librovisor, Ediciones Alternativas del Centro Cultural de Espana en Guatemala, p. 288.

Arrivillaga Cortés, Alfonso (1988). «Apuntes Sobre la Musica de Tambor entre los Garifuna de Guatemala». *Tradiciones de Guatemala,* 29, 57-88.

Arrivillaga Cortés, Alfonso (1988). «Introduccion a la Fenomenologia y Organologia de la Musica de Tambor entre los Garifuna de Guatemala». *Tradiciones de Guatemala,* 30, 75-94.

Arrivillaga Cortés, Alfonso (1990). «La Música Tradicional Garífuna en Guatemala». *Latin American Music Review/Revista de Música Latinoamericana,* 11 (2), 251-280.

Arrivillaga Cortés, Alfonso (2010). «La Punta: un Ritmo para Festejar la Nación Garífuna» in Albert Recasens Barbera y Christian Spencer Espinosa, (ed.) *A Tres Bandas, Mestizaje, Sincretismo e Hibridación en el Espacio Sonoro Iberoamericano.* España: Editorial AKAL, pp. 139-150.

Arrivillaga Cortés, Alfonso (2010). «Del Tambor Africano a la Música Garífuna. Un Recorrido por las Formas Musicales y Danzantes de los Garínagu». *En Clave Afrocaribe.* Guatemala: Agencia Española de Cooperación Internacional, pp. 62-93.

Arrivillaga Cortés, Alfonso (2010). «Andy Palacio camino a seiri: un homenaje». *Patrimonio Cultural Centroamericano,* 5 (5), 10-12.

Arrivillaga Cortés, Alfonso (2010). «El Garawoun Sonando la Nación Garífuna». *Patrimonio Cultural Centroamericano,* 5 (5), 18-29.

Beals, Paul W. (ed.) (1964). *Nijein Uremu Tidan Nanigi (There is a Song in my Heart). Gospel Songs and Choruses.* Central America: Nazarene Mission.

Ben, Yee (2007). «A Contrapuntal Look at Punta and Punta Rock, a Garifuna Cultural Mezcla(sh)» <http://yeeality.

com/blog/a-contrapuntal-look-at-punta-and-punta-rock-a-garifuna-cultural-mezclash/>.

Cayetano, E. Roy (1977). «Garifuna Songs of Mourning". *Belizean Studies*, 5, 17-26.

Cosenza, Antonio (1987). *Die Traditionelle Musik aus Livingston/ Izabal/Guatemala fur Garaon (Trommel) Chichira (Bassel) und Gesang*. Schriftliche Hausarbeit für DML,University of Hamburg.

Crisanto Melendez, Armando (1988). «El Garifuna, su Folklore en Honduras» in *Primer Congreso de la Cultura Negra de las Americas*. Cali, Columbia: UNESCO / Fundacion Colombiana de Investigaciones Folkloricas, pp. 89-92.

Crisanto Melendez, Armando (1997). *Adeija Sisira Gererun Aguburigu Garinagu» El Enojo de las Sonajas; Palabras del Ancestro»*. Tegucigalpa: Graficentro Editores.

Crisanto Melendez, Armando (1997). *El Enojo de las Sonajas. Palabras del Ancestro*. Tegucigalpa: Graficentro.

Dirks, Robert (1976). «John Canoe: Ethnohistorical and Comparative Analysis of a Carib Dance». *Actes du XLIIe Congres International des Americanistes*, 6, 487-502.

Espinal, Mario (1994). *Tambores: Expresiones Artísticas del Pueblo Garífuna*. Tegucigalpa: FOSOVI.

González Cajiao, Fernando (1994). «Loubavagu: Entre la Tradicion y la Vanguardia». *Latin American Theatre Review*, 28 (1), 153-158.

Greene, Oliver N. (1998). «The Dügü Ritual of the Garinagu of Belize: Reinforcing Values of Society Through Music and Spirit Possession». *Black Music Research Journal*, 18 (1-2), 167-181.

Greene, Oliver (1999). *«Gender Roles and Spirit Possession in Garifuna Society: The Use of Music for Ancestor Worship*. Ph.D. Thesis, Florida State University.

Greene, Oliver, Jr. (2002). «Ethnicity, Modernity, and Retention in the Garifuna Punta». *Black Music Research Journal*, 22 (2), 189-216.

Hadel, Richard (1972). *Carib Folk Songs and Carib Culture.* Ph.D. Thesis, The University of Texas, Austin.

Hadel, Richard (1974). «Words of Some Carib Songs». *Belizean Studies,* 2 (6), 26-30.

Hadel, Richard (1976). «Black Carib Folk Music». *Caribbean Quarterly,* 22 (2and3), 84-96.

Jenkins, Carol and Travis Jenkins (ed.) (1981). «Garifuna Tape Collection Notes (Barranco 86-105-F, OT6955-58 Seine Bight 86-105-F, OT6959-60 Hopkins 86-105-F, OT6961-64 Dangriga Series I 86-105-F, OT6965-75 Dangriga Series 86-105-F Notes on Dugu and Bibliography Notes for Sample of Garifuna Music 81-087-D transcription of tapes in Garifuna with English translation.)» Belize unpublished.

Jenkins, Carol L and Travis Jenkins (1982). «Garifuna Musical Style and Culture History». *Belizean Studies,* 9 (6), 6 -12.

Johnson, Guion Griffis (1937). *Ante-Bellum North Carolina: A Social History.* Chapel Hill: University of North Carolina Press.

MacMillan, Douglas (1926). «John Kuners». *Journal of American Folk Lore,* 39 (151), 53-57.

McGranahan, L. (2008). «Play, Jankunu Play: The Garifuna Wanaragua Ritual of Belize». *Ethnomusicology,* 52 (2), 339-341.

Murillo Selva Rendon, Rafael (1997). *Loubavagu, o, "El otro lado lejano».* Versiones Garífuna y Español.* Tegucigalpa: Editorial Guaymuras.

Penedo, Ismael and Leonardo D'Amico (2000). «La Culture Musicale des Garifuna, Communauté Afro-Amérindienne d'Amérique Centrale». *Cahiers de Musiques Traditionnelles,* 13, 65-75.

Perry, Marc D. (1998). «Garifuna'z in the Hood: A Musical Making of a Hip Hop Identity». Presented at the University of Texas African Diaspora Conference.

Shedd, Margaret (1933). «Carib Dance Patterns». *Theatre Arts Monthly,* 17 (January), 66-77.

Stone, Michael (2008). «Diaspora Sounds from Caribbean Central America». *Caribbean Studies,* 36 (2), 221-235.

Taylor, Douglas MacRae and Harvey C. Moore (1948). «A Note on Dominican Basketry and Its Analogues». *Southwestern Journal of Anthropology*, 4 (3), 328-343.

Twiss, Horace (1819). *The Carib Chief: A Tragedy.* London: Longman, Hurst, Rees, Geme, and Brown.

Vincensini, Cyril (2006). «Tambours Africains, Voix Amérindiennes: Les Caribes Noirs d'Amerique Central». *Nuevo Mundo Mundos Nuevos*, <http://nuevomundo.revues.org/1794>. Consultado el 05 enero 2011.

Whipple, Emory (1971). *Music of the Black Caribs of British Honduras.* Master of Music Thesis, The University of Texas at Austin.

Whipple, Emory (1976). «Pia Manadi». *Belizean Studies*, 4 (4), 1-18.

Whipple, Emory (1979). *Modernization and Music among the Garifuna of Punta Gorda, Belize.* unaccepted Ph.D. Thesis, Indiana University.

Wilson, Samuel M. (1991). «Saint George and John Canoe». *Natural History*, 100 (December), 22-27.

Spirituality / Spiritualité / Espiritualidad

Arana, Pietra (1993). *Lemesi Lidan Garifuna.* Belize: self published.

Beaucage, Pierre (1991). «Le Catholicisme et les Garifonas du Honduras». *Recherches Amerindiennes au Quebec,* 21 (4), 67-76.

Bianchi, Cynthia Chamberlain (1988). *Gubida Illness and Religious Ritual among the Garifuna of Santa Fe, Honduras: An Ethnopsychiatric Analysis.* Ph.D. Thesis, Ohio State University.

Brett, William Henry (1880). *Legends and Myths of the Aboriginal Indians of British Guiana.* London: W. W. Gardner p. 206.

Chamberlain de Bianchi, Cynthia Maria (1979). *Ritual Possession Trance and Ancestor Illness among the Garifuna of Honduras: An Analysis of the Gubida Cult.* M.A. Thesis, Louisiana State University.

Chamberlain de Bianchi, Cynthia Maria (1984). «La Enfermedad de Gubida y el Sincretismo Religioso entre los Garifunas: Un Analisis Etnosiquiatrico». *América Indígena,* 44 (3), 519-542.

Concilio Cristiano Garifuna, (1994). *Weremuja lun Bungiu.* La Ceiba, Honduras.

Crisanto Meléndez, Armando (1991). «Religious Elements of the Garifuna Culture and their Connotations in the Americas» in Kortright Davis and Elias Farajajé-Jones (ed.) *African Creative Expressions of the Divine.* Washington, D.C.: Howard University School of Divinity, pp. 121-127.

Crowe, Frederick (1850). *The Gospel in Central America: Containing a Sketch of the Country.* London: C. Gilpin.

Flores, Barbara Anne Therese (2001). *Religious Education and Theological Praxis in a Context of Colonization: Garifuna Spirituality as a Means of Resistance.* Ph.D. Thesis, Northwestern University/Garrett-Evangelical Theological Seminary.

Flores, Barbara (2002). «The Garifuna Dugu Ritual in Belize: A Celebration of Relationships» in Rosemary Radford Ruether (ed.) *Gender, Ethnicity, and Religion: Views from the Other Side.* Minneapolis: Fortress Press, pp. 144-172.

Flores, Justo (no date). *Lau Furiyeigui Luma Teremu Liguilisi.* Los Angeles: self published.

Flores, Justo (no date). *Turagate Mariya Luguchu Bunguiyu Garifunau.* Los Angeles: self published.

Flores, Justo (1979). *Furumiye Katekisimu Garifunau Anglaisi Luma Chumageu.* Los Angeles: self published.

Foster, Byron (1982). «An Interpretation of Spirit Possession in Southern Coastal Belize». *Belizean Studies,* 10, 18-23.

Foster, Byron (1983). *Marriage in Death: Ritual Representations of Belizean Garifuna (`Black Carib') Society.* Ph.D. Thesis, Unverisity of Cambridge.

Foster, Byron (1987). «Celebrating Autonomy: The Development of Garifuna Ritual on St. Vincent». *Caribbean Quarterly,* 33 (3-4), 75-83.

Foster, Byron (1994). *Heart Drum: Spirit Possession in the Garifuna Communities of Belize. 2nd Edition.* Belize: Cubola Productions.

Genon, S.J., Jean (1871). *Lemerina Ciel: Pasos al Cielo.* Roeampton: Manresa Press.

Gullick, Charles J.M.R.C. (1988). «Chamanismo Garifuna». *America Indigena,* 48 (4), 283-321.

Hopkins, Frederick C. (1918). «The Catholic Church in British Honduras (1851-1918)». *Catholic Historical Review,* 4 (October), 304-314.

Howland, Lillian G. (1984). «Spirit Communication at the Carib Dugu». *Language and Communication,* 4 (2), 89-103.

Howland, Lillian G. (1988). *Communicacion con los Espiritus en el Dugu Garifuna (Caribe).* Guatemala City: Instituto Linguistico de Verano de Centro America.

Idiáquez, Jose (1994). *El Culto a los Ancestros en la Cosmovisión Religiosa de los Garífuna de Nicaragua.* Managua: Instituto Historico Centroamericano.

Idiáquez, Jose (1982). *El Culto a los Ancestros en la Cosmovisión Religiosa de los Garífuna de Nicaragua.* Managua: Instituto Historico Centroamericano.

Jenkins, Carol (1983). «Ritual and Resource Flow: The Garifuna» Dugu». *American Ethnologist,* 10 (3), 429-42.

Johnson, Paul Christopher (2002). «Migrating Bodies, Circulating Signs: Brazilian Candomble, The Garifuna of the Caribbean, and the Category of Indigenous Religion». *History of Religions,* 41 (4), 301-27.

Johnson, Paul Christopher (2002). «Models of "The Body" in the Ethnographic Field: Garífuna and Candomblé Case Studies». *Method and Theory in the Study of Religion,* 14 (2), 170-195.

Johnson, Paul (2004). «Migrating Bodies, Circulating Signs: Brazilian Candomblé, the Garifuna of the Caribbean, and the Category of Indigenous Religions» in Graham Harvey and Charles D Thompson Jr. (ed.) *Indigenous Diasporas and Dislocations: Unsettling Western Fixations.* London: Ashgate, pp. 38-51.

Johnson, Paul Christopher (2005). «Three Paths to Legal Legitimacy: African Diaspora Religions and the State». *Culture and Religion,* 6 (1), 79-105.

Johnson, Paul Christopher (2007). «On Leaving and Joining Africanness Through Religion: The "Black Caribs" Across Multiple Diasporic Horizons». *Journal of Religion in Africa,* Berkeley 37 (2), 174-211.

Johnson, Paul Christopher (2007). *Diaspora Conversions: Black Carib Religon and the Recovery of Africa.* Berkeley: University of California Press.

Kerns, Virginia (1980). «Garifuna Women and the Work of Mourning (Central America)» in Nancy Auer Falk and Rita M. Gross (eds.) *Unspoken Worlds: Women's Religious Lives.* San Francisco: Harper and Row, pp. 123-125.

Lumb, Judy (1996). «Garifuna Dugu: A Really Extended Family Reunion» <http://www.judylumb.com/dugu.html viewed 2 December 2011>.

Macklin, Catherine L (1972). *Aspects of Black Carib Religon.* B. A. Thesis, Harvard University.

Macklin, Catherine L (1976). «The Garifuna Thanksgiving». *Belizean Studies,* 4 (6), 1-5.

Muir, Deborah (1996). «Two Priests: One People». *The Reporter,* 17 November 1996 Issue, 4.

Palacio, Joseph O. (1973). «Carib Ancestral Rites: A Brief Analysis». *National Studies,* 3, 3-8.

Sered, Susan Starr (1994). *Priestess, Mother, Sacred Sister: Religions Dominated by Women.* New York: Oxford University Press.

Sletto, Jacqueline Wiora (1991). «Ancestral Ties that Bind». *Americas,* 43 (January/February), 21-27.

Sociedad Bíblica de Honduras, (2001). *Sandu Burutu.* Tegucigalpa, Honduras.

Sociedades Bíblicas en Centro América, (1966). *Le Meja Jadugubei Lounagulegu Jesusu.* Guatemala.

Staiano, Kathryn Vance (1991). «The Dugu: Health and Healing in Garifuna Societies». *The World and I,* 6 (1), 660-670.

Suazo, Salvador (2000). *Irufumali: la Doctrina Esotérica Garífuna.* Tegucigalpa: CEDEC/CORDAID.

Tourism / Tourisme / Turismo

Aguilar, Juan Manuel and Sergio Antonio Palacios (2003). *La Ciudad de Trujillo: Guía Histórica Turística.* Tegucigalpa: Instituto Hondureño de Antropología e Historia.

Braun, Jessica (2008). *Community-based Tourism in Northern Honduras: Opportunities and Barriers.* Honors in Environmental Studies Thesis, University of Manitoba.

Brondo, Keri and Laura Woods (2007). «Garifuna Land Rights and Ecotourism as Economic Development in Honduras' Cayos Cochinos Marine Protected Area». *Ecological and Environmental Anthropology,* 3 (1), 2-17.

Cuisset, Olivier (2009). «Tourisme et Garifunas à Livingston, Guatemala: Economie et Culture en Contexte Touristique». *Documento de Trabajo No. 7 / Document de Travail No. 7,* Proyecto AFRODESC, <http://www.ird.fr/afrodesc/IMG/pdf/Cuaderno7 -Cuisset-2.pdf> viewed 4 January 2111.

Cuisset, Olivier (2010). «Exotisme et Folklorisation: Tourisme et Culture Garifuna à Livingston, Guatemala». *Rita,* 3. <http://revue-rita.com/traits-dunion-thema-51/exotisme-et-folklorisation-thema-133.html> viewed 4 January 2111.

Duarte, Kurt Fortin (1997). *GIS Tools for Development of Honduras Tourism.* M.A. Thesis, National Central University, Republic of China (Taiwan).

Eguchi, Nobukiyo (1994). «Ethnic Tourism and the Caribs' Recreated Ethnicity: A Case Study on the Relationship between Tourism and Culture in the Caribbean». *Ritsumeikan Journal of International Relations and Area Studies,* 6 (March), 113-132.

Key, Carol Jane (2002). *Cayes, Coral, Tourism, Ethnicity, Belize.* Ph.D. Thesis, University of North Texas.

Kirtsoglou, Elisabeth and Dimitrious Theodossopoulos (2004). «"They are Taking Our Culture Away": Tourism and Cultural Commodification in the Garifuna Community of Roatan». *Critique of Anthropology,* 24 (2), 135-57.

Kirtsoglou, Elisabeth (2008). «Se Estan Llevando Lejos la Nuestra Cultura»: Turismo y Comercializacion de la Cultural en la Comunidad Garifuna de Roatan». *Yaxkin*, 24 (1), 67-81.

Lucey, Mark (1993). «Recommendation and Evaluation for the Toledo Village and Guesthouse and Ecotrail Program of the Toledo Ecotourism Association» presented at the School for International Training Belize Program.

Rédiger la Biographie

Carlson John Tuttle est né en Amérique du Nord. En 1967, il est diplômé de l'Université de Windsor dans le Windsor, en Ontario. C.Tuttle a également fréquenté l'Université d'Etat du Wayne, l'Université d'Etat du Michigan et l'Université de l'Ouest de l'Ontario ainsi que d'autre universités de l'Etat du Michigan. Carlson John Tuttle est membre de la Southern Highland Craft Guild depuis 1983 et enseigne à la John C. Campbell Folk School depuis 1988. Actuellement, il est le seul au Belize à pratiquer encore certaines techniques de vannerie traditionnelle garifuna comme la fabrication de la ruguma (presse à manioc). En 1986, il s'installe à Barranco, dans le sud de Belize, où il fonde trois ans plus tard la Tuani Garifuna Tuba Liburu, une bibliothèque de recherche en anthropologie sur la culture garifuna. Depuis sa création, Carlson y tient le rôle de bibliothécaire de recherche. En 2011, il coécrit avec Joseph Palacio et Judith Lumb *Garifuna Continuity in Land: Barranco Settlement and Land Use 1862 to 2000*.

Escriba Biografía

Carlson John Tuttle nació en América del norte. En 1967 es diplomado de la universidad de Windsor en Ontario. C. Tuttle ha igualmente frecuentado las universidades estatales de Wayne, de Michigan y la Universidad de Ouest en

Ontario así como otras universidades de Michigan. Carlson John Tuttle es miembro de la Southern Highland Craft Guild desde 1983 y enseña en la John C. Campbell Folk School desde 1988. Actualmente es la única persona en Belice que practica todavía ciertas técnicas de cestería tradicional garífuna como la fabricación de la ruguma (para exprimir la yuca). En 1986, Carlson Tuttle se radica en Barranco — sur de Belice — donde funda tres años después la Tuani Garífuna Tuba Liburu, una biblioteca de investigación antropológica sobre la cultura garífuna. Desde su creación Carlson se desempeña como bibliotecario de investigación. En 2011 participa, con Joseph Palacio y Judith Lumb, en la publicación del libro *Garífuna Continuity in Land: Barranco Settlement and Land Use 1862 to 2000.*

Author Biography

Carlson John Tuttle is of North American heritage. In 1967 he graduated from the University of Windsor in Windsor, Ontario. Carlson also attended Wayne State University, Michigan State University, the University of Western Ontario and various campuses of the University of Michigan. Carlson has been a member of the Southern Highland Craft Guild since 1983. He has taught at the John C. Campbell Folk School since 1988. Carlson is the only person who still makes ruguma (cassava squeezer) and other traditional Garifuna basketry in Belize. In 1986 Carlson moved to Barranco in the south of Belize where he founded three years later the Tuani Garifuna Tuba Liburu, an anthropology research library on the Garifuna culture. From its founding, Carlson has been the reseach librarian of this library. In 2011, Carlson co-authored with Joseph Palacio and Judith Lumb *Garifuna Continuity in Land: Barranco Settlement and Land Use 1862 to 2000.*

www.ingramcontent.com/pod-product-compliance
Lightning Source LLC
Chambersburg PA
CBHW030336270326
41926CB00010B/1646